YOUR UNANTICIPATED DIVORCE

Holistic Healing Strategies and Suggestions

Dr. Milton Michael Kobus

ISBN 978-1-64471-700-4 (Paperback)
ISBN 978-1-64471-701-1 (Digital)

Copyright © 2019 Dr. Milton Michael Kobus
All rights reserved
First Edition

All rights reserved. No part of this publication may be reproduced, distributed, or transmitted in any form or by any means, including photocopying, recording, or other electronic or mechanical methods without the prior written permission of the publisher. For permission requests, solicit the publisher via the address below.

Covenant Books, Inc.
11661 Hwy 707
Murrells Inlet, SC 29576
www.covenantbooks.com

For all those victimized by an unanticipated, undeserved divorce who are determined to heal.

CONTENTS

Acknowledgment 7

Prologue 9

Chapter One: Quo Vadis? 21

Chapter Two: Suggestion Therapy 97

Chapter Three: How to Get Off the Couch 167

Chapter Four: Really Loving Yourself 207

Epilogue 267

ACKNOWLEDGMENT

Complete gratitude is given to each of my healed colleagues, family, and friends whose anguish, determination, and wisdom have inspired this book.

My most sincere appreciation is proffered to the creative agency of the Triune God.

PROLOGUE

I *was* the victim of unanticipated and undeserved divorce. Directly stated, if this machination has also been your plight then my concise book is written for you. Its assumed anticipation is that you profoundly desire to heal from the tragedy of your absolutely undeserved, unexpected, unforeseen divorce(s). A healthy holistic method of practical unanticipated divorce healing *suggestions* will be proffered for your benefit within this treatise. It is designed to provide a variety of provocative recommendations and strategies to both incite as well as expedite your healing process. Since much of unanticipated divorce healing is contingent upon the reader's attitude and effort, the work refuses to offer a guarantee of success. Any endorsement promoting the surety of success without actually knowing its reader would be preposterous. However, this book will certainly present sincere and reasonable proposals for healing from experienced veterans who have survived and eventually thrived as a result of their determination to heal from an unanticipated divorce. Consequently, this work is the mentally agonizing result of the devastating experiences encountered by the author and a series of contributing colleagues. I have been blessed

Prologue

to interview these insightful and astute women and men each of whom were once angry and despondent yet today are psychologically robust.

The majority of divorce healing recommendations, strategies, and *suggestions* presented in the following pages emanate from the anguished grief of people much like you. In short, the proposed *suggestions* revealed throughout the following chapters, may serve as a solid template for you to gradually and prudently create your own private and personal divorce healing propositions. However, most determined readers will no doubt strongly consider and utilize the practical advice proposed by experienced "survivors" within these pages.

Since the healthy holistic healing of an unanticipated divorce is a gradual process involving one's entire being (body, mind, and soul) it is logical to move forward immediately. It would be irrational for the reader to endure even one more day of anguish and frustration. Hence, within the following paragraphs eight introspective questions designed to aid the incipient healing process by reflection on the status of your former marriage will be introduced. As you assiduously reflect upon your past adversity you will receive the necessary attitudinally dependent impetus to progressively attain a healthy future. These questions are the point of departure for all those genuinely committed to healing from the consternation of their undeserved and unpredicted divorce. While pertinent and most probably relatable they may evoke an emotional response. Yet whatever

Prologue

may be your emotional reaction the intent of these introspective queries is for you to focus not on loss but rather on incipient progress.

Often those who deeply desire healing from an unanticipated divorce become static and ensnared by a quagmire brimming with anger, confusion, and frustration resulting from their personal tragedy. They tend to lose intellectual clarity regarding the stark reality and true nature of their former marriage. This aimless ruminating can be the result of being embroiled within a current state of continuous disorientation. It becomes akin to running a treadmill—expending energy with no forward progress. They may rationalize or romanticize the abhorrent event, which appears to have unhinged their life ad infinitum.

Hence, it is obligatory for a provocative prologue to interpose clarification into the conundrum. A stringent exposition will serve as a reasonable and responsible harsh reminder of that which must be absolutely relinquished. The upcoming questions are focused on that outcome. They should bring the reflective reader to certain obvious understandings which are frequently deferred due to personal guilt or complex obfuscation. Therefore, it is obligatory for that determined reader to seriously consider the following compellably probative truisms prior to responding to an upcoming series of introspective seminal questions.

Prologue

1.) As difficult as it may currently appear, you must succumb to the stark reality that your marriage has been terminated by another's narcissism and selfish decision.
2.) The opportune moment to move forward with your new life has now commenced.
3.) While change is inevitable, its ramifications are contingent upon your attitude.
4.) You draw meaning for your life from no other human person except yourself.
5.) Positive healthy growth can be developed from negative events and experiences.
6.) Allow your former marriage to become both a teaching and learning moment.

With the above assertions in mind, this prologue invites you to profoundly engage the following eight questions. Having completed this pertinent exercise, the author will provide you with a brief analysis of his personal unanticipated divorce experience. The intent will be to illustrate a genuine unexpected divorce situation with which the reader can possibly relate. Early on in the divorce healing process it is both exigent and prudent to resonate with the travails of others who have experienced similar sufferings which you currently endure. This identification generates an indispensable path toward the reality that your personal trauma, while daunting, is virtually identical to the cognitive dissonance overcome by a host of others in the unanticipated divorce healing community. Therefore, in a place and time of

Prologue

solitude profoundly reflect upon each of the succeeding questions.

Did you, like me, have an intensely loving marriage? Did your marriage, like mine, seem to be flowing quite smoothly? Despite the natural occurrences of life, did your marriage also provide you with a palpable sense of mutual reliance and frequent whimsy? Did you, like me, often feel the comfort and solace of a healthy fulfilling marital relationship? Did your spouse, children, home, and lifestyle provide you, as it did me, with a sense of peace in the silence of the day's end? Did you, like me, know that while others possessed more "stuff," you and your spouse had the fullness of one another? Did you, like me, believe that something sacred dwelt within the beauty of your marriage? Finally, were you, like me, absolutely devastated when your now former spouse astonishingly insisted upon the necessity of an unexpected divorce?

If you answered "yes" to the above questions then *you today, were me, some years ago*. For like you, the person to whom I had completely given myself surprisingly no longer loved or even wanted me in her life. When this insidious declaration was delivered there seemed to be no words to express the utter disappointment and phenomenal despondency that overwhelmed my very being. Naturally, I foolishly condescended to pleading for her love. This humiliation then developed into my egregious bargaining for us to somehow remain together. The rejection of this desperate and final proposition then morphed into my personalized guilt. I obsessed over a futile yet penetrating self-analysis attempting to specifically determine which of my behaviors had created her heinous demand. Finally, in the throes of the totality of my confusion, I became polarized by an awkward type of vitriol, a love/hate dilemma. Hence, while I pleaded out of blind ignorance for reconciliation, simultaneously, my anger drilled down into a hatred for her and acrimony for the euphoric relationship which she chose to desecrate.

Ironically however, I was still willing to change anything about me for her. Yet I was perplexed by a culpability that was imperceptible. Certainly, I did not mean to insinuate my personal perfection but what unknown fault had suddenly overshadowed me? Neither did I genuinely comprehend what needed to be altered within me in order to remain with her. Naturally, perhaps like you, I tearfully begged friends to intercede. Of course, most of them felt awkward and did absolutely nothing to help mediate the situation as they were intent upon confronting their own demons.

In time, an eerie depressive attitude had soon become my diabolic companion. Illusion toyed with my mind as I focused solely on the fantasy of reconciliation. Yet in rare lucid moments came the grim realization that "the die had been cast." I was aware that her life was continuing to move forward while I was drifting away from my very self.

Oddly, I eventually considered myself to have been allocated into a novel albeit unpleasant demo-

Prologue

graphic profile. I emerged as a self-ordained "residual." I had been abruptly abandoned. I had been callously disposed of by another. I was a discarded leftover. I became the unwanted residue of a formerly sublime marriage.

If the reader recognizes this abhorrent proclamation and is able to resonate with it then *you are what I once was*. Consequently, I ask an indulgence to engage in a brief yet critical diversion from my catastrophic narrative as this is a kairotic (most opportune) moment.

This subsequent interlude is designed to alleviate the reader from a frequently toxic notion common to incipient divorce healing progress. These particular introductory remarks will refer to this pernicious disposition as "the residual syndrome." Much more on this debilitating syndrome's effect will be treated in subsequent chapters. However, at this initial state of your divorce healing process, with unabashed honesty interrogate yourself, asking, "Do I really consider myself to be a residual"? If so, while erroneous, even this condescending admission can truly initiate your personal divorce healing process. However, be advised that it is an absurd acknowledgment. You absolutely know that you were not created to live as a leftover entity. Profoundly and continuously focus on this healthy self-recognition as you develop.

You have now identified your personal point of departure. I am proud of you for having placed yourself upon the precipice of a new life. You are just beginning to reject a formerly inaccurate self-perception while anticipating a new valid and appropriate perspective. Having seized the moment with an intentional interruption (a flaccid admonition) I respectfully continue my personal scenario. You are exigently encouraged to persist in an assiduous examination of your particular scenario while reading through the balance of this revelatory prologue.

Briefly delving into my perceptual field during the inchoative periods prior to a providentially tailored unanticipated divorce healing enterprise will not be a feckless endeavor. There will be considerable value in avoiding a cavalier or cursory reading.

Throughout my youth, I had received the gift of a strong spirituality from my parents. Hence, raising my family with a sincere belief in a loving God was a cherished responsibility. We held fast to weekly church attendance. The Bible maintained a prominent place in our modest library. We received the sacraments at the appropriate times. A Sunday reception of the Eucharist was both desirable and obligatory.

However, this unanticipated divorce compelled me to confront a personal problem of evil. I prayed with fervor for God to eliminate and revoke this unexpected suffering. Yet no reconciliation or revocation appeared and the divorce was finalized. Over time and with considerable anger I rejected the God whom had seemed to reject me.

Those infamous "irreconcilable differences" banished me from my loving family and comfortable home. Due to a lack of funds, the necessity of child support, and everyday bills, I was forced to move

Prologue

into a hovel in a sketchy neighborhood across the city. Here, I merely existed. Feeling sucked into the vortex of a claustrophobic abyss I was being engulfed into some enigmatic black hole. Like an automaton, I thoughtlessly trekked between my job and the frigid emptiness of an intolerably secluded one room flat. My work colleagues tried to encourage me with their foolish views of my new found "freedom." They could not realize my lack of freedom. I had become a slave to the bondage of abjection, anger, and angst.

I now errantly reasoned that since I was "a residual" (see above) rejected by God, my spouse, and friends a new lifestyle must be adopted. Perhaps, solace might be found in mingling with others of my ilk. The local pubs would become my new houses of worship. I was careful to keep sober. I was careful in my spending. I was most careful in the observation of desperate people forcing themselves to party into temporary oblivion. Yet the diabolic beckoning of "Scylla and Charybdis" was most alluring, enticing, and titillating. However, after a significant but temporary *faux pas*, the cogent realization eventually concluded that I could no longer swim in that cesspool.

Since no one seemed to care about me, I began to gradually take stock of myself. It had become emotionally exhausting to sit and stare aimlessly at cold empty walls. I was bereft of any physical exercise. I had no real intellectual stimulation. My spirituality had atrophied. I had allowed myself to become one holistic disaster. I was gradually becoming sick and

Prologue

tired of being sick and tired. Somehow, something deep within kept imperceptibly stirring and prompting me toward a palpable desire to feel better about myself.

I determined that the least expensive and most beneficial activity was for me to walk every night. With these steps I did not realize then that my divorce healing was about to begin. As I walked, I talked to myself and concluded over time that I was much more than "a residual." In some numinous way I felt an intense determination to gradually become a healthy and healed person. I recognized that it was incumbent upon me to discover, unpack and alter any issues which were debilitating that burgeoning determination. In sum, despite all of the undeserved and unanticipated divorce metrics which were reducing my self-esteem, I painstakingly refused to consume myself with these diabolic notions.

Here I choose to conclude this intimate, proprietary, and revelatory prologue.

In the following pages, the reader will be exposed to a variety of both explicit and subtle divorce healing concepts, recommendations, strategies, and *suggestions*. These have truly motivated me and many others with whom I have interacted to heal from the anguish of an undeserved, unexpected, and unforeseen divorce.

If you meticulously study this concise book, prepare yourself for an enlightening personal self-discovery as well as the holistic progress obligatory for your desired divorce healing. Determine today that you are absolutely not "a residual." Gradually, adapt an inclination toward self-motivation and self-respect never allowing your personal authenticity to be "discarded" by anyone. Realize the strength of your God-given bona fide self-worth. Know that you are entering both a new secular and sacred venue. Do not attempt to circumvent the divine assistance which awaits your interconnectivity within the purview of a holistic spirituality. Prepare your disposition for a transformation through this holistic divorce healing process.

Stringent considerations of these introductory motifs will be explicated in detail throughout the following sequential chapters. Study each with an open mind and an attitude oriented toward your healthy divorce healing through probative strategies. Now, is the opportune moment to move forward by an astute examination of the treatment proffered in subsequent chapters.

A mandatorily transparent disclosure to the *cynical* reader is compulsory at this juncture. The above introduction has hopefully stimulated a further study of this manual. However, since I have freely shared much of my initial unanticipated divorce experiences for your benefit no duplicity will be camouflaged. Hence, while living in the shadow of my first "unhealed" divorce, I embarrassed myself by participating in another marriage to a decent and attractive person. Errantly, I allowed myself to succumb toward "macho inclinations" and her physical attraction without having a genuine comprehension

Prologue

of the healthy holistically spiritual healing process. This turbulent, non-sacramental, non-valid or licit, one year marriage ended with another unanticipated and undeserved divorce. *I was not* the common denominator of these two annulled and unwarranted divorces. My only anguish from the very brief second marriage was pecuniary and definitely self-embarrassing. These are the real issues, which nearly 60 percent of second divorce situations must confront. The work produced in this treatment is based primarily on my first marriage.

Ultimately, all of these heavy-hearted eventualities, with God's grace have assisted my unanticipated divorce healing and encouraged the necessity to write this book. I have now been very happily married for many years. I prayerfully request that the triune God's divorce healing grace fill the heart and mind of each reader as they *study and apply* the recommendations, strategies, and *suggestions* proposed in the following chapters.

CHAPTER ONE

Quo Vadis?

Where are you going? This chapter opens with *the* most pertinent and perturbing question necessary to be addressed by every resolute member of the unanticipated divorce healing community. "*Quo vadis*"—where are you going? Are you currently an affiliate of this anguished assembly who is profoundly determined to heal from the vitiating effects of an unconscionable, undeserved, unexpected, and unsupported divorce? Then it is absolutely expedient to truthfully confront this personal inquiry at the inception of your divorce healing enterprise. So where *are* you going? Have you been asking yourself this disquieting question since the tragic incipience of your unanticipated divorce? Consciously and perhaps even subconsciously has this inquiry haunted the very core of your being? Has it violated the secret sanctuary of yourself so deeply that frequently you wonder, "What has become of me?" Has this perplexing query dominated virtually every moment of your quotidian existence? Do you hold a cavalier attitude toward your other responsibilities being mesmerized solely by this confounding question? Do you occasionally find yourself without direction merely sitting and aimlessly staring into space?

The introductory paragraph compels and insists on a conscientious clarification, "*quo vadis*"—where are you going? How are you going to answer this impelling question? Or does your dismal response unfortunately consist of a feeble desire to just make it through the night? Are you going to allow this muddled attitude to modulate your currently flummoxed and disoriented lifestyle?

If you can resonate with the above questions and are perplexed by an intellectual paralysis, this is not uncommon. The previous paragraphs can be disconcerting because they insinuate the necessity to address issues at the very core of your being. Most people "believe" that they possess an awareness of where they are going in their lives. However, this assertion is generally true if one conceives of her or his life's direction as being only driven by the material and superficial. Once, one enters into the more profound realm of the most fundamental consequential concerns of life, angst begins to permeate one's thinking. This leads either to complete avoidance or an existential fear. From infancy, we have become quick study's in the area of avoidance, i.e., a fight-or-flight tendency.

However, for most members of the unanticipated divorce community, it is fear that has become an uncomfortable bedfellow. We all fear the unknown, particularly when it challenges us to accept and "work through" new phenomena. In this venue, one will discover specifically what the "*quo vadis*" question immediately requires. Scarcely do any human persons want to admit that they have lost their sense of direction in life. Further, it is an additional denigration to realize that this situation allows your former spouse, in some manner, to control your attitude and focus. Your anger, confusion, frustration, and interior pain are being manipulated by the one who used to fulfill you. This persists in an unusual cyclic fashion, which only vitiates your ability to heal. Your resentment is further complicated by the realization that your former spouse is not even cognizant of her or his dominance in the recesses of your mind.

In an oddly bizarre sense you are being errantly puppeteered by an obsessive nostalgia. It has been both my experience and that of many others that these emotions and issues become normalized when unanticipated, undeserved divorce healing appears remote. If these obstacles seem insurmountable, it may provide you with some solace to know that others have succeeded in overcoming them. Hence, as difficult as it may currently appear, your acceptance of the responsibility to eliminate perniciously meandering thoughts regarding your former spouse is within your control. This will be one of many invaluable *suggestions* proffered to you in the following chapters. To paraphrase the Christ, living in fear is a useless waste of psychic energy. Faith is the necessary virtue which will allow you to receive a new and strategically determined answer to your "*quo vadis*" question.

The ramifications caused by the trauma experienced as a result of your unanticipated divorce are naturally quite devastating. They debase your personhood even further if mastery over yourself appears to be obfuscated. However, the incongruity which astonishingly comes to immediate fruition is that ironically you are actually experiencing the incipient stage of your divorce healing! Therefore, a consequence of this cataclysmic event will allow you a choice. You are absolutely free to remain lost and capriciously hope for the emergence of some illusory directive. Or you may conceive of this tragedy as an opportunity for your personal renaissance. It is at this potential point of departure that only you can elect to designate just where you prefer to be going and how to arrive at the appropriate destination.

It is a dire prognostication to indicate that you are assuredly emotionally drained and physically exhausted. You subsist as an addled victim of your undeserved, unforeseen divorce. Family and friends have riddled you with feckless advice which only adduces additional complex pressures. In general, your sense of trust has been virtually depleted.

Each of the above issues is endemic to your current posture at the incipience of the divorce healing enterprise. It is extremely commonplace to endure these untenable positions at those initial "moments" following your unforeseen divorce. This is most frequently the nascent condition of flustered victims just entering into the unanticipated divorce community.

A stringent strategic plan conjoined with your holistic spirituality will free you from this nefarious treadmill. Obviously, this is a metaphorical piece of exercise equipment designed to keep you running with increased speed but without any real sense of destination. For purposes of this book, your holistic spirituality is the God-given gift whereby the human person utilizes her/his body, mind, and soul to collectively communicate and interface with the triune God. The proper use of these component elements of one's being conjoins the human spirit with the infinite, unconditioned, unrestricted, omnipotence of the Holy Spirit. When used appropriately in faith the divorced victim will heal more efficaciously and expeditiously from the devastation of an unanticipated divorce.

Considerably more will be explicated regarding your holistic spirituality throughout this concise volume. You have been graced with the free agency to gradually move from darkness into light. Should you choose progression, as with most life altering processes, anticipate certain difficulties related to the general human (Adamic) condition caused by the effects of the Original sin. Simultaneously, know that you possess the capacity to effectuate divorce healing opportunities. Negative situations can provide positive results when strategically directed. Hence, there should not be a scintilla of doubt that the recommended strategies and *suggestions* in this handbook can provide your life with a healthy sense of divorce healing direction. However, your obligation is to adamantly seek the grace to enact the grace of the God-given freedom with which you have been graced.

If you acutely aspire to earnestly heal from your unanticipated divorce then a radical commitment to this resolution is requisite. Do not allow yourself to think myopically regarding the oft-used term "commitment." A sincere commitment is only as valid as its maker. It is much more concerned with your personal optics. The existential threat of your divorce is concluded. Where do you now seek to go? Demonstrate your determined commitment to the above resolution by a meticulous study of this concise yet pertinent manual. With no sense of cynicism open-mindedly consider its holistic *suggestions*.

Recall, a holistic *suggestion* considers your entire being through the lens of your holistic spirituality in the divorce healing process. You will assertively utilize the God-given gifts of your body, mind and soul to mitigate your lack of direction and move toward healing. Simply stated, the use of your entire being in this holistic manner can realistically bring your divorce healing to fruition. Hence, if the previous inquiries of the introductory paragraph leave you deficient of reasonable and responsible answers then you must choose where you are going.

A comprehensive exposition of your "holistic spirituality" is compulsory in the thorough understanding of this divorce healing process and will now be recapitulated. Despite any personal reservations that you may currently hold in reference toward God the following paragraphs are imperative for your introspection.

The reader needs be advised that although this is not a theology text the crux of your healing will ultimately be the result of your active relationship with the divine Trinity (in prayerful exercises of your whole being.) Recall, however, that the purpose of this book is to offer practical strategies and *suggestions* designed to help you heal from an undeserved, unexpected, unforeseen divorce. However, the prospect of your divorce healing is substantially enhanced through the application of a holistic method. This, therefore, implies the necessity to use your "wholeness of being" to fully heal. When this wholeness is thoroughly examined the three-fold distinction of your humanity is revealed.

As a human person you are composed of a human body, a human mind and a human soul. Hence, your body is your personal physicality. It is the temple of the Holy Spirit. Your mind and its various faculties is the cognitive aspect of your being. It is a finite version of God's omniscience. The soul is your animating principle created specifically for you in the image and likeness of God. When these three elements of your human personhood are conjoined and mutually operative, in an interactive communicative process with the triune God, this unified whole is your "holistic spirituality." It generates its existence from a freely gifted relationship with the Trinitarian God. Specifically, the completeness of your spirituality is actually life in the Holy Spirit. This Holy Spirit is the absolute, unrestricted love which God the Father and God the Son have for one another. Hence, in order for your divorce healing to genuinely occur the unabated "use" of your holistic spirituality is mandatory.

It is logically incontestable to seek real divorce healing without appropriating all efficacious opportunities. In this context, it is respectfully necessary to realize that the Trinitarian God is not a supernatural device which exists to mechanically produce your utilitarian desires. However, people of all religious denominations, have petitioned and received God's unrestricted assistance. Astonishingly, God is encouraging you to ask, seek, and entreat the omnipotent, omniscient, remediation which awaits your divorce healing opportunity. The God who loved you into existence anxiously desires to heal you from all the agony resulting from your unforeseen divorce.

Therefore, the anticipation of your current desires for both divorce healing and new found happiness will result from a relationship with the only Being that can truly provide for those specific needs.

It is a fundamental and innate drive for all human persons to seek happiness. It is equally fundamental and inherently human to seek "The Transcendent More." Consequently essential to the human heart and mind is the pursuit of "The Ultimate." This is an elementary component of a general yet real theological anthropology. Hence, it may be viewed as the natural human orientation toward God which is revealed through the body, mind, and soul.

Yet theology is faith seeking understanding. In attempting to achieve this transcendental understanding some degree of happiness is naturally viable. Humanity longs for a comprehension and relation with that which is greater than itself. This is a documented aspect of the historicity of humanity. Some may reference this reality as "the sacred source of unconditional love." Others may consider this reality as "the ground of all being." However, terminology aside, including the specificity of an appellation like "God," this unique reality is the first cause of one's holistic spirituality. This holistic spirituality allows us to respond to the calling of a relationship with the triune God.

It is the height of prudence to procure the omnipotent Love and unrestricted Wisdom of the Trinitarian God as one seeks advancement toward the divorce healing proposition. Your personal spirituality is God's gift to facilitate an unconditional loving relationship directed toward you. Holistic healing promotes the reality that your spirituality is as authentic and irrefutable as your personality and character traits. With God's infinite love, the grace of your holistic spirituality, and the practical *suggestions* in this book you are essentially within the throes of a healthy and "whole" divorce healing progression. Abrogating this spiritual nexus with the triune God, however, allows you to do nothing! This assertion is axiomatic for your unanticipated, undeserved divorce healing.

Some additional amplification and more precise explication of this concept regarding your "holistic spirituality" may be further warranted. Since you are the architect of your own life, it is expedient to attain a thorough comprehension of this divinely (yet very human) gracious benevolence. Your God-given holistic spirituality, which includes the human body, mind, and soul that you have possessed since conception is not some form of chicanery to be identified with a natural avoidance, escapism, or suppression.

Obviously, all rational members of the unanticipated divorce community, desire to avoid dwelling upon the consternation prompted by their divorce. Clearly, it is equally natural to mentally (and perhaps, physically) escape and/or suppress the recurring anguish inflicted upon you by the narcissistic initiator of this catastrophe. However, holistic spirituality moves well beyond these very natural and mundane defense mechanisms while never negating their existence.

The proper utilization of the God-given, unmerited, and unwarranted componential gifts of your body, mind, and soul are oriented toward the Creator by their very nature. You may conceive of this axiomatically as a theological anthropology. For example, your body is the Temple of the Holy Spirit. Your mind is the intellect and will which you finitely possess as a reflection of the infinite intellect and will of God. Your soul is where you are most deeply rooted in the creative act of existing in the image and likeness of God through emotions, freedom and self-awareness. Therefore, to reiterate, in the context of this treatment, holistic spirituality is not about avoidance but rather about the acceptance of a given reality. Neither, is it about escapism but rather the embracing of painful events and experiences then learning from them through your insight and the Wisdom (Jesus Christ) of the triune God. Nor is your holistic spirituality about suppression but rather about a Phoenix-like ascension and revelation. In sum, it is the appropriate exercise of each human component within both a conjoined interconnection and a faithfully interactive relationship with the unconditional love and omnipotence of your God who desires to help direct you toward unanticipated divorce healing. This is the essence of your holistic spirituality in terms of the daunting "quo vadis" inquiry.

The above consideration of the realities concerning an unconditionally loving assistance by God and/or your personal holistic spirituality may be vehemently rejected by some readers. If this is your quandary, it is understandable, however, try to be open-minded as the following elucidations will be informative no matter what disposition you may currently maintain.

Your current state of being may subsist within massive amounts of non-specifically directed anger, confusion and frustration. Your emotional condition may be intensely acerbic for quite a while. You may begin to demonstrate a somewhat truculent personality. You may hate God for "allowing" your divorce to occur. Furthermore, you may even deny the existence of a God who would permit such evil to enter your life. Some may lay this book aside considering the above assertions as mere pious platitudes or religious placeboes. Intractability can be a mendacious bed-fellow.

If the above exemplifies your current contention, then *you are today where I once was*. As the prologue to this book indicates, I rapidly became disgusted with the God that I had once worshiped. In vitriolic criticism, I categorically denied the existence of such a pernicious God. I struggled to comprehend how any good could come from this evil predicament ordained by this God.

Consequently, in a virtually infantile tantrum, I explicitly disdained any notion of God or my supposed spirituality. *If* this is the situation in which you are presently immersed, know that many victims of divorce have also errantly held these identical suppositions. Yet with no intent to offend an emotionally distressed reader, based on my experience, your anger at God is irrational. It may take some time and profound introspection based on your genuine holistic spirituality for you to make the quantum leap which leads to the realization *that your former spouse (not God) is responsible for your unanticipated divorce.* For some untoward reason, your unanticipated divorce was expedient to satiate the deceptive, lustful longings, and narcissistic inclinations of a self-centered spouse.

The penchants of your former spouse are/were beyond any logical rebuttals, which you possess. Leave those issues to the omniscient and forgiving God. However, do not allow yourself to run afoul, rife with a fallacious conclusion whereby you deny *both* the existence of God and your holistic spirituality. This misconstrued thinking is a preposterous enterprise. These two realities not only exist but are absolutely essential to your undeserved, unforeseen divorce healing. You know that you are much more than pure physicality. You also know that you possess a mind which allows for variant cognitive processes. Additionally, you know that are animated by a God-given soul. These three conjoined aspects of your being are your holistic spirituality. Further, all three are not self-generated rather they are specifically created by God for you. A denial of their existence is illogical. Plants and animals are also living entities which have a body, are sentient instinctual reactors and are animated by a type of soul. However, you are filled with spiritual aspects and attributes that they can never possess. For example, you know that you know that you know that you know. You are aware of your being aware. Only a divinely "spiritualized" being is capable of this mode of cognition.

You are created with a soul finitely made in God's image. Your holistic spirituality is your direct connection with that loving creator God. You have been graced with an intellect, a will, freedom, and human emotions which are components of your soul. While each is non-palpable, you know that they are as real as your personality, intelligence and character traits. Your anger, confusion, and frustration will subside in due course with a determined effort and a sense of faith in yourself and the Holy Spirit. Focus on persistence in relaxation rather than debilitating your psychic energy. Gradually allow the unconditionally loving God's direction working within your timeframe and holistic spirituality to provide a sense of divorce healing guidance.

Recall that this concise manual is not intentionally a thesis on spirituality. Yet it can be the perfect point of departure to begin the process of healing from your unanticipated divorce. You must first heal from within. Hence, the denial of the spiritual components which connect you with God only delays and debilitates your opportunity to move forward. Therefore, respecting the reader's current status, your choice is either to let anger continue its control and domination or to accept the realities that will recreate a healthy and healed "new" you.

Later chapters will tease out both direct and indirect holistic healing *suggestions*. In point of fact, the astute reader may have already become aware of a plethora of recommendations and *suggestions* commencing the healing process. However, future *suggestions* will be very pragmatic being grounded in both secular and sacred realities. Therefore, since they will be holistic it is exigent that some will involve basic physical activity to release your endorphins and other peptides. Still others will evoke a critically essential intellectual and "soulful" stimulation obligatory in the refocusing of your overall thinking. This is intended in order that the determined reader will quickly ascertain a dynamic sacramentality, which is revealed in your healthy holistically spiritual divorce healing process.

Be advised, as you continue to study there will be multiple references to the triune God and your holistic spirituality. Understand that the primary concern of this book is not *necessarily* your conversion; although, you will gradually observe a palpable correlation between your holistic divorce healing and a more profound reliance on the Trinity.

Simultaneously, the focus of the strategies and *suggestions* is not merely to provide a "sanctified" method for you to *cope* with the trauma of being victimized by your divorce. The objective is to provide you with proven *suggestions* for a healthy holistic healing from an unexpected divorce. Hence, you must initially treat this pain and suffering from within the core of your being. The purpose is not succumbing to the frequent temptation of only treating the symptoms. Your holistic spirituality in collaboration with God's unconditionally loving omnipotence will laser focus on the appropriate cure. Herein lays the only authentic method for you to heal.

At this juncture, it is once again essential to briefly clarify some common misconceptions regarding holistic spirituality. The absolutely critical nature of this reality for the unanticipated divorce healing community member must be acknowledged. Your holistic spirituality is only tangentially related to holiness or saintliness. It is not necessarily about church traditions and worship or about being a devoutly religious person since we all are sinners. *However*, there is definite merit to each of these delineations. It most certainly does not exclude any of these inclinations or modes of being.

Holistic spirituality, intentionally considered in this work is viewed as a condition of every human nature. It is innate and globally ubiquitous to all human persons as we are "graced" to possess the gifts of a body, mind and soul. These conjoined aspects of your human nature are not self-begotten. They are the freely given gifts of the unconditionally loving God directed to your specific personality. You apprehended these gifts at your conception. You were not conceived as a *tabula rasa*. Throughout the gestation period and thereafter, you, as Christ Himself, grew in wisdom, age, and grace.

The point of the respective above assertions regarding your holistic spirituality is this: by using the wholeness of your spirituality you exponentially increase the prospects of your holistic divorce healing. This is the direct result of a human and a divine interconnectivity between you and the Holy Spirit. The Holy Spirit is the third person of the Trinitarian God consubstantial and co-equal in every way with the Father and the Son. The Holy Spirit proceeds as the infinitely joyful explosion of love between the Father (the first divine Person) and the Son (the second divine Person).

If you are not healed from your unanticipated divorce this is because your nexus with the Holy Spirit has not yet been properly utilized. Divorce healing is neither vapid nor for the faint of heart. This is another reason to sharpen the relationship between you and the Holy Spirit. The reader will, at best, find only temporary relief without the loving advocacy of the Holy Spirit. Hence, you can never expect genuine divorce healing without the direct involvement of your holistic spirituality with God, the Holy Spirit.

It is affirmed, once again, that the complete utilization of your body, mind and soul (which is your holistic spirituality) is absolutely compulsory if you are to heal thoroughly from your divorce. With due respect and humility addressed to the reader, holistic healing *suggested* in this concise book will "dovetail" flawlessly with your holistic spirituality as explicated throughout the various sequential chapters.

Recall your body is the temple of the Holy Spirit. Whether woman or man you are infused with the very DNA of the triune God. Your (weekly) reception of the Eucharist as the true and real body, blood soul and divinity of the glorified Christ further acknowledges and reinforces this dogma. Those who view "holy communion" as the potent symbolic memorial event unifying humanity to Christ are obliged to partake of this bread and wine as profound spiritual nourishment aiding the divorce healing process.

At this inchoate period of your development while the aggregate of new concepts can be overwhelming try to purge yourself of any lingering skepticism. It is blatantly understood that being skeptical, at this juncture, is not an unwarranted assumption since your trust factor has been temporarily severed. Yet consider that the mysteries which are being considered in your study are visible signs of the invisible presence of the Holy Spirit. You stand at a defining moment in your life. You do possess the God-given freedom to reject the above assertions and continue your current lifestyle. Yet with no sense of sarcasm, this chapter encourages you to ask if "your plan has been effective?" If it is not, then, opt to trust in the authentic Truth of the Holy Spirit, who beckons you at this very moment. Realize that the Holy Spirit is the breath of God residing within you as the first cause of your holistic spirituality. Accepting this inspirational breath of the triune God, you will have a new and crisp creativity. "The Divine Counselor" who is longing to provide therapeutic healing from the pain of your divorce will proffer a viable plan conducive to healthy emotional stability. This emotional injury cannot heal itself with flaccid direction and a tenuous strategy. *Ergo*, do not concoct your own divorce healing!

As the reader is aware, the pain of healing may frequently be more severe than the endured injury. Since each of us is a corporeal being (with a spiritual component) we naturally heal at different rates and various degrees based on physical and psychological factors. However, now is the perfect moment to employ your nascent proactivity. You can no longer be a reactive victim. It is the opportune time (the kairotic moment) for you to proactively rely upon the Wisdom, Understanding, and Counsel of the Holy Spirit to assist with direction and guidance. This synthesizes as a result of the appropriate integration of your holistic spirituality in tandem with the Holy Spirit. Direction and guidance are frequently elicited by the Holy Spirit through other people, situations, and the commonplace experiences occurring in your daily life. If you can faithfully acknowledge these notions, then progress is manifesting itself in your unanticipated divorce healing.

Being fully cognizant of your current maturational phase, consider the following illustration of possible holistic activities (prayerful exercises) in conjunction with the genuine holistic spirituality which you possess. You will find this to be an uncomplicated and effective daily procedure.

1.) Use your body in some endorphin releasing physical exercise(s). For many, like this author, daily walking (at one-half hour) is inexpensive, healthy, and a prayerful event. Caveat: your choice of a physical activity is contingent upon the athletic prowess and health status which you possess. Prudent judgment is your ally, however, do not tend toward lethargy. Ask your doctor if so warranted.
2.) Stimulate your mind by choosing a favorite intellectual pursuit. A "good read," a

movie, a challenging game, listening to music, can all be a prayerful experience raising your heart and mind to God while also mitigating depressing thoughts. Your mentative life is a demonstrative prayer honoring God and your entire being.

3.) Your soul not only animates you but also involves the intellect, emotions, freedom, and will. Candid "soulful" expression, either in angered prayer to God or while seeking divine direction is a necessity in your unanticipated divorce healing. Resolve to freely and honestly communicate with your Creator by speaking and also aggressively listening.

Even, the skeptical reader is capable of determining the holistic value of the above exercises as boding well for the human person. Now, when these three componential entities are unified they form a potent method to assist your divorce healing process. The objective, although not obligatory, is to activate them concomitantly. Hence, in the above illustration, as you walk or work out nothing can prevent your opportunity to engage in healthy thoughts and multiple styles/expressions of prayer. The entire procedure is further amplified by intentionally and verbally interconnecting these holistic pursuits within a passionate and candid communication with the Holy Spirit. As can readily be observed, the beauty and simplicity of the *daily* utilization of your holistic spirituality is neither cumbersome nor time consuming. It is truly a God-given benefit contingent upon your "whole" determination to actualize an inherent divorce healing potential.

If you ruminate over the above illustrative example and then enthusiastically actualize it, much psychic energy will be preserved. Through a quotidian and thorough utilization, you will develop and refine this "healthy, healing habit" and recognize its validity and virtue. A gentle "tongue-in-cheek" admonition to the cynical, skeptical, or obdurate reader is now warranted: do not reject God's persistence in this venue unless your current strategy is candidly generating phenomenal healing results!

Recall, this chapter is proffering solid, proven strategies and *suggestions* to help you answer the "*quo vadis*" question. Once this has been identified and then begins to gradually entertain some realistic response, you are now beginning to progress in your unanticipated divorce healing. Hence, whatever may be your current status regarding the plight which you continue to endure, be assured of the following axiomatic assertion. Your determination to heal from an undeserved and unexpected divorce while fundamental and necessary *is not sufficient* to provide enough real-life direction and thoroughly continuous healthy healing. Very respectfully, it is little more than the proverbial Band-Aid solution to a deep wound which requires a truly cooperative patient being treated by the "divine physician." If you, wherever you may be in your experienced personal tragedy, can accept, acknowledge and activate the above potent truth then this indicates a positive movement in the divorce healing encounter.

Without appearing scurrilous and with no intent "to throw shade" if anger and skepticism continue to abrogate your unanticipated divorce healing development conscientiously examine the consequent stringent observations.

You possess the immense capability to truncate the tutelage offered by The Holy Spirit by intractably resisting the exercise of your holistic spirituality. If you are attempting to generate a determined divorce healing by your own processes a cascade of turbulent emotions/feelings will soon emerge. This is the natural result of utilizing your already perturbed lifestyle to self-prescribe an effective and healthy healing remedy. It is a *non-sequitur* to believe that if one is currently psychically depleted, that individual may advance a psychic antidote efficacious in the profundity of a life altering condition like divorce healing. Without the appropriate use of one's conjoined natural and supernatural healing venues (strategic holistic spiritual exercises and a faithful intercommunicative relationship with the triune God) any solo effort becomes a foolhardy enterprise! Simply stated, every person determined to genuinely heal from an unanticipated divorce must accept non-interfering direction from God and simultaneously exercise each component of her/his holistic spirituality. No prudent medical professional or concerned caregiver would prescribe aspirin to heal a lethal carcinoma.

Quo Vadis?

However, despite the above logical certainty, many incipient and/or intractable members of the unanticipated divorce community believe that they can control their "situational status" by thoughtful well intentioned schemas. These individuals like a large number of previously divorced veterans, although in the throes of a misdirected anger, confusion, and frustration still desire to forge their own unique path to renewal and ultimate healing.

While credit is given for worthwhile intentions and the definite ability to make highly intelligent mundane decisions, in the realm of this chapter's propaedeutic question, good can readily become the enemy of the great. For what appears, feels, or seems to be the correct course chosen is often counterintuitive toward the substantive nature of an actual healthy personal development which bonds the finite and infinite together in a "whole" strategic, definitive, and directional solution. This, then, is the incipient healing strategy, which can move even the most reluctant believer toward initial healing progress. A glimpse toward a proactive response to your "*quo vadis*" question is now dawning.

Prior to moving forward, however, it is both compassionate and mandatory to briefly treat the excruciating misery experienced by vast numbers of the unexpected and undeserved divorce healing community who had discovered marital infidelity. This untoward situation often becomes the rationale (albeit errant) for their recalcitrance in accepting the reality of holistic spirituality. Female or male, they remain emotionally devastated and frustrated not knowing where to truly direct their profound pent-up anger.

To reiterate, this immature and selfish violation of the sanctity within your marriage was not caused by God but rather by the free choice of a despicable and narcissistic person. It was the ultimate insult to you, which revealed the latent sexual promiscuity initially unobserved in those early perceptions of and romantic interludes with your former spouse. Consequently, it is almost beyond sensible articulation to share this deplorably heinous and egregiously freely chosen sexually insidious behavior(s) with another human being. The loathsome, perverse, and stealthy duplicity necessary to denigrate one's marriage cannot be coherently expressed. If this was a condition of your previous marriage, logic reminds you that it was not the decision of the unconditionally loving God. It was the free but unconscionably selfish choice of your weak former spouse enjoyably succumbing to temptations while unconcerned with your (and your family's) devastation. In the slanged idiom of one healed divorce survivor, "You dodged a bullet from a fully loaded gun."

As grotesque and highly offensive as the above catastrophic event has been for many of us, there is a challenging but real solution. It is promulgated in terms of the "*quo vadis*" question. You are now an absolutely free agent. You have been painfully freed from the depths of anguish, constant anxiety, and inexpressible tension which accompanied this terminated "marriage." At great emotional expense, you are now truly able to become the one person who determines your own destiny. Recognize, that the proper utilization of your God-given holistic spirituality conjoined with the necessity of emotional prayer for healing direction, will gradually mitigate (then eliminate) any pain and provide a new sense of reference. This novel reference point can, if you choose to believe and activate it, allow much of life's current turbulence to subside and redirect your mind-set.

Indifference to all aspects, concerns or curiosities regarding your former spouse must now become the critically salient "safe word." Much more will be delineated on the importance of *indifference* toward any activity of your former spouse provided within the following chapters. However, begin to appropriate this term into your daily reflections and routine unanticipated divorce healing self-speak.

As with much of the holistic divorce healing enterprise, there is substantive benefit to self-reflection. It is ingredient toward providing some initial release from the catastrophic effects elucidated by of your divorce. For example, if your former spouse was sexually unfaithful, profoundly reflect upon the following somewhat acerbic rhetorical questions.

1.) What do you candidly believe would be more beneficial to your authentic personal happiness: either being "married" to an unfaithful spouse or finding a new and healthy direction for your life?

2.) Can you change the antics and mind-set of an unfaithful spouse?
3.) Are you able to live normally together with this perversion continually haunting your mind?
4.) Knowing all that you now know, was your unanticipated divorce a curse or a blessing?

At this point, take the above four questions through a trial exercise of your holistic spirituality. While introspecting upon these rather stringent issues, here (in this example) is the opportune moment to release endorphins by using your physicality. Now is the opportune moment to exercise your intellectual ability through logical, rational thought, producing an effect on the mind and not necessarily eliciting a reply. Now is the opportune moment to engage your soul in an emotionally passionate prayer expressing anger and frustration while concurrently seeking Trinitarian directives.

The reader should hopefully be asking whether this holistically spiritual approach (as simply delineated) is not vastly more advantageous and effective than merely sitting alone with idle non-directed, non-conclusive scattered thoughts. The answer is obvious and deliberately demonstrates the facility of your holistic spirituality in action. The above exercise, if meticulously followed, will draw the perceptive reader ever closer toward an authentic response to your "*quo vadis*" question.

Given the above, an assiduous study of this chapter's initial segment is revelatory in both the necessity and comprehension of your holistic spirituality. Since repetition is the mother of learning, recall again, the relevant definition of holistic spirituality for the audience to whom this concise manual is addressed. (Concurrently realize that holistic spirituality is gifted to all human persons and should be at the core of *any* relationship between humanity and God.)

Your holistic spirituality is that specific God-given gift (grace), which requires the appropriate utilization of one's body, mind, and soul in profound interrelationship with one another and the Trinitarian God. The purpose of this gift can be multifaceted, however, the application with which we are here consumed is the healing of one victimized by an unanticipated, undeserved divorce. The actual utilization or intentionally focused exercise of each component (body, mind, and soul) is not only absolutely necessary to this healing process but is also a prayer, i.e., a communicative experience with God. This prayer should be considered as a kind of "active utterance" combined with an aggressive listening to the triune God, the ground of all being. Prayer may be formatted in terms of adoration, thanksgiving, forgiveness, and petition to The Holy Unconditionally, Unrestricted, Infinitely, Loving Creator of all that exists.

The circumstance of unanticipated divorce naturally most often encourages prayer of petition. This reality is necessitated by the need for an answer to the "*quo vadis*" question as well as assistance and direction to counteract the effects of lingering anger, confusion, and frustration. However, in the most proper prayerful exercises of the body, mind, and soul, one is not attempting to escape post-divorce related issues or concerns. Rather, if the holistic approach is correctly utilized, one is petitioning through each component for a healthy change (a strengthening of attitude, a diminishment of anger, a sense of direction) to occur within *one's self*. Therefore, even in the depths of heartfelt communication with God, the fullness of prayer found throughout holistic spirituality does not seek a change in God's behavior or Holy Will. For this would be a preposterous contradiction in terms of God's immutability. Rather, your holistic spirituality seeks a healthy change of mind and heart (a metanoia) within you to accept the providential direction of God during both composed and turbulent times.

Prior to continuing these assertions regarding the accurate expectations of prayer, brief consideration should be given to the issue of God's ability to miraculously "change" the entire reality of your divorce's occurrence. Many neophytes in the experience of unanticipated divorce healing pray that God, with whom all things are possible, earnestly respond to this desperate supplication. The question then may become: can you pray for God to work a miracle in *reference* to your unanticipated divorce? This question is complicated, not for God, but for you. What does this specific miracle entail on the part of God? If one means will God reverse the historical event of your divorce—i.e., will God change an actual past, previously occurred historical phenomenon? This would be a contradiction which is unreasonable to consider since it would anticipate a violation of the free will of your former spouse and of forward aggregating temporality.

God's miracles in the realm of healing the blind, the lepers, and commonplace daily miraculous events requires deep faith in addition to prayer but are essentially inexplicable. God's thoughts and ways are not our thoughts and ways. Hence, everything which is not a contradiction of reality or the creation of evil, is possible for God, e.g., God cannot create a circled-triangle of the same area in the same respect at the same place and time. Consider another provocative query: suppose that two high school teams vying for the championship trophy adamantly pray to win their Friday night game which team will God support? The team with the most points will win. This is not a supernatural issue; however, God is always honored by humanity's prayer.

Consequently, the "miracle" for the victim of an unanticipated divorce is found in her/his ability to change through prayer accepting God's healing direction in accord with one's activated holistic spirituality. Hence, when you ask, seek, or knock for God's direction, the real petition (and miracle) is to accept God's Will in your overall healthy, healing progress. *The miraculous occurs in your daily acceptance since you are being changed!* If you aggressively listen, a burgeoning answer to your "*quo vadis*" question is miraculously coming to fruition.

Recall, your holistic spirituality, as a member of the unanticipated divorced community, is not about a child-like avoidance, escapism, or suppression of reality. Rather, it is about utilizing your body, mind, and soul in a healthy manner as a potent prayerful exercise. It is not about physical, mental, or soulful diversion or sublimation. Your holistic spirituality is about an aggressive posture to confront, with God's direction, the remnants of anger, confusion, and frustration diabolically trying to negate divorce healing progress.

This progress initiates with your determination, faith and desire to holistically heal and specifically answer the "*quo vadis*" question for yourself. This unrelenting determination, itself is originally initiated by the grace of God. You need God's grace to petition and seek God's grace. God's consummate providence is ubiquitous and manifold in an omnibenevolent concern for your overall well-being.

How do you know where you are going? The answer is found in holistically prayerful petitioning God in a daily plainspoken candid conversation whereby sincere speaking and aggressive listening occur concurrently. The goal is for you to change in accordance with God's perfect Will. Recall, we are made in God's image and likeness. The reverse is not the case.

It would be the height of normalcy at this point for the reader to ask, "In what manner are my body or mind or soul, while being exercised, considered to be prayer?" Provocatively analyze each component of your whole being while assiduously considering the following responses. Recall, that authentic prayer comes in variant forms.

However, it is always sincere communication (active speaking and aggressive listening) with the Trinitarian God. Its ultimate objective is to conjoin your will with God's Will.

The exercise of your *body* (as one holistic component activity) is indeed a prayer in the subsequent manners.

A.) It is a grace from God uniquely chosen from an infinite number of possibilities.

A grace is not only God's favor but also God's self-communication. The prayerful communication of thanksgiving to God for both your very existence and ability to utilize this body (whatever may be its physical prowess) is an act of devotion.

B.) Your body is the temple of the Holy Spirit. In the physical exercise of this body, you are demonstrating prayerful worship of your Creator who abides deeply within your being.

C.) For the unanticipated divorce victim, physical exercise on any endorphin increasing level, prayerfully "calls out" as an utterance, a groaning that strains against demonic lethargy. This utterance and straining is a form of bodily worship offered to God in terms of one's physicality. It is akin to a yogi, an aboriginal dancer, and many forms of Asian, African, and Native American gestured meditative prayer. The physical exercise of your body, then, is an outward manifestation of communicative prayer to the Designer, Creator and Sustainer of this incredible human body with which you have been graced (i.e., grace as God's self-communication). In God's infinite Wisdom, God chose to create us as physical (not angelic) human beings (not automatons or AI) and for our salvation Christ took on a specific human body in the incarnate Word (the self-revelation of God.)

D.) As another God-given gift of the exercise of your body, take notice that it is virtually impossible to remain in the doldrums if you throw yourself into rigorous exercise. This bodily exercise strengthens you while simultaneously honoring God. Your body was created by God not to exist in an inert state but to prayerfully illustrate its power as a finite reflection of God's omnipotence.

Quo Vadis?

The exercise of your *mind* in the realm of holistic spirituality is prayerful for multiple reasons.

A.) Your mind's mentative activity is the genesis for all forms of prayer. This includes the affective and cognitive applications of prayer to God regarding adoration, thanksgiving, forgiveness and petition. One caveat, which the reader will discover below, is that prayer is not of necessity always a pious declaration. The human mind "contains" many nuances which include prayer directed to God in anger, frustration, and lamentation (e.g., most Old Testament Psalms). These emotional communications between the human and divine are deeply prayerful.

B.) Your mind is the locus of directions from God as well as the source for a multiplicity of insights. These "insights" include, but are certainly not limited to, appreciation of beauty, resolution of problems, applications of mathematics and physics, planning for your future, experiencing la joie de vivre, praying to comprehend God's healing directives, etc. Further, your mind is the incisive instrument by which you come to an experience of The Sacred, a dynamic form of prayer.

C.) Your mind is prayerful as the center of the conscious self-awareness which you currently possess and which will develop through healthy, healing cognitive experiences. Consider the reality that appropriate exercise of your finite mind is a prayerful honoring and a faithful mirroring imitation of God's preeminent intellectual mentations. Akin to the continuous creative agency of God, your finite creative and intellectually stimulating thoughts (including prayer) are a microcosm of God's activity. Your prayer is a mentative creative communicative exercise which is reflective, responsive, and interactive within God's self-communication.

D.) Your mind allows thoughtful change to occur as you pray for divorce healing progress. You prayerfully focus your mind on change from negative emotions and thoughts to positive healing alternatives. The reader should consider that it is only through your mind that genuine divorce healing will occur in cognitive cooperation with God's communications. The parameters, the determining factors of your divorce healing are guided by a healthy attitude, daily exercises of holistic spirituality, and candid quotidian communication with God.

E.) A prayerful change in your thinking will result in a prayerful outcome. This is especially true in the unanticipated divorce healing enterprise, whereby a prayerful alteration in your mental outlook will provoke a prayerful change of mind and heart. The change of your mind-set can only occur through an alteration within the mind's focus. This is a challenging task, which can only be accomplished by a determined mind prayerfully seeking God's unconditionally loving direction.

F.) The peace of mind which surpasses all human comprehension, a necessity in the unanticipated divorce healing process, is a prayerful gift from Christ to you. Christians of all denominations prayerfully assert this aspiration at each Mass or prayer meeting memorializing Christ's gift of His peace to all humanity.

The exercise of your *soul* as one component of the holistic spirituality, which you possess is a prayerful act for the following reasons:

A.) If prayer is candid communication (unreserved speaking and aggressive listening) with and from God, then it is mandatory in terms of authentic expression. Since you are created in God's image (the soul) there is an open linear innate interaction and interrelation which can only be fulfilled in prayer oriented toward that Creator. You bring your entire self (in anger or belligerence, euphoria or jubilation) to God in "soulful" prayer. Recall, that since God is immutable you are not "hurting" God in angered soulful expression of honest prayer. In fact, you are gradually and positively being changed each time that you emote in soulful prayer toward the unconditionally loving God. The reader must never assume the posture that God is either stoic or petulant and only aridly concerned for any expressions of your communication. Your soul participates in the very nature of God through the unfathomable gift of God's real presence during reception of the Eucharist. Hence, your weekly reception of the true and real body, blood, soul, and divinity of Christ is the "nourishment" necessary for the soul's health. A symbolic memorialization in "holy communion" provides the spiritual food and unity of purpose by the congregation to help form a personal union with Christ. In either prayerful event, lies the ultimate earthly opportune moment between you and God, the consummately prayerful time for your soul's thorough communication with its Creator. As a member of the unanticipated divorce community, your emotional strength stems from a potent relationship with God, fully activated and nourished by a soulful prayer life.

B.) As you consider the "*quo vadis*" question within the context of your divorce healing process, remain fully cognizant of the soul's yearning for God. Your soul is inherently longing for frequent communication (prayer) with the God who actually thought it into existence. This communication may come as you find God in other people, circumstances and the daily occurrences of your life. In certain specific situations, God's unexpected insight or inspiration may emerge instantaneously. This or any communication by the triune God requires a prayerful response. Therefore, again the communicative interaction between your soul and God is fittingly exercised.

C.) Recall, that the soul's prayerful communication with God can be more than mere petition. The soul's yearning for God is also expressed in prayer of adoration, forgiveness, and thanksgiving. As can be readily envisioned, human articulation is insufficient to separate the exercise of the soul, the mind, and the overall sense of spirituality. Hence, the reader should try not to confuse your unique God-given soul with the concept of personal spirituality. While there is a semantic relationship, your soul by its nature involves the ensemble of intellect, will, emotions and freedom. It is a spiritual entity. Spirituality, however, is a holistic activity which "umbrellas" body, mind, and soul. Yet without the soul's interaction, prayer is an impossible enterprise.

By now the diligent (and perhaps, somewhat perplexed) reader is asking, "Why does it matter if each component of my holistic spirituality is a prayer since I desire only to be healed from the anguish of my unanticipated divorce?" Consider the following responses to the above query.

1.) Without these three holistic components how will you communicate with God?
2.) Without each of these activated components, how will God communicate with you?
3.) The exercise of each component not only strengthens your divorce healing but also prayerfully seeks God's Wisdom in the process.
4.) While prayerfully accepting and utilizing these componential gifts, you also prayerfully accept the divine assistance of The Giver.
5.) How else can you genuinely heal without physical, mental, and soulfully exercised prayer to The One who will change your perspective on both yourself and the implications of the unforeseen divorce?

Suffice to say, that the clarifications on the holistic components as prayer when appropriately exercised, are neither convoluted nor esoteric propositions. When these nuanced delineations are validly considered and applied they are highly plausible and probatively definitive. This conclusion is derived from their practicality and usefulness by many former victims who are now healthy holistic "survivors" healed from an unanticipated divorce. Your engrossed abstraction of these holistic exercises as the type of communication with God which will strengthen this divorce healing process must be conscientiously introspected. Hence, whatever may be your current deliberations in reference to the reality of the multiple proposed postulates covered within this chapter consider the following. Compose yourself enough to logically acknowledge *both* the presence of a holistic spirituality subsisting within you and God's non-interfering omniscient providential guidance.

Throughout the above treatment the reader will notice that the denigration of "professional therapy" is never discouraged. In point of fact, a good Christian therapist, for some individuals seeking overall divorce healing, can be beneficial. If you have the energy, money, and time combined with the belief that this directive is God's Holy Will (never impinging upon your free choice) this approach can be valid. However, be assured that either directly or indirectly a quality Christian therapist will be engaging you at some level of your holistic spirituality.

This method of therapeutic engagement is absolutely essential to your divorce healing.

Counterpoising this situation is the reality that many members of the unanticipated divorce community do not possess the energy, time or financial wherewithal to work with a professional therapist. In the active pursuit of a marital annulment, a priest (or minister depending upon your religious denomination's protocol) may be of considerable assistance. However, this may or not be genuinely therapeutic during your incipient healing development. Hence, as you continue to study, do not downplay the significance of the *suggestions* found in this concise book as a genuinely potent instrument for your divorce healing. In fact, it will provide exceptional preparatory research either prior to or in conjunction with a professional therapist or psychologist. A simple caveat: study this manual before succumbing to impulsive alternatives.

At this particular juncture, the reader may now be asking, "when will these supposed divorce healing *suggestions* be shared?" The specificity of this question authentically demonstrates, in a healthy manner, a vibrantly anticipated concern to know just "where you are going." Further, a given reader may conclude that the previous material, while somewhat beneficial, is proffering only a limited sense of direction. If these thoughts are even vaguely representative of your current posture, be at ease. What you are embarking upon is the requisite proactive lifestyle alluded to previously. You want some cathartic action to occur. This is exceptional news which serves to illustrate that you are eager to redirect your life. You are beginning a more profound alternative response to your unanticipated divorce healing. Your enthusiasm is gradually unfolding. This is a classic example of a negative stimulus leading to a positive response. Recall, the earlier proclamation that you are not "a residual," you are now gradually acclaiming your determined healing desire and self-worth. You are incipiently reaching a point of critical mass by resisting negative acceleration.

The necessary caveat in your enthusiastic declaration is twofold. The first concern regarding the healing *suggestions* is answered below. A variety of reasonably subtle *suggestions* have already been proffered initiating with the prologue's remarks shared in this manual. The majority of these *suggestions* have usually been presented in the form of rather docile imperative sentences. Others are formatted as directly assertive statements (e.g., God is not responsible for your divorce, rather, that responsibility is focused on the free choice of your former spouse). It will be highly beneficial to review and redline these as salient points for a more thorough study. Also, it is always an asset to one's recollection to write personal notes in the margins of a given page.

Secondly, the next chapter will unpack a number of specific and therapeutic *suggestions* gleaned from the healing experiences of astute veterans (now survivors) of divorce healing. The reader should be advised, however, that even this author had frequently tripped over himself in a frantic attempt to impetuously snare the healing process and force its occurrence. Recognize that this is not the route of genuine holistic divorce healing. We have all been conditioned, perhaps programmed, by an overtly hurried culture to expect rapidity in all our eventualities. Consequently, it is quite plausible that a cavalier or skeptical reader may simply wish to peruse the *suggestions*, abruptly evaluate their worth, use some, negate others, and hope to immediately dive into divorce healing. Obviously, this is a perfunctory strategy.

Prudence dictates that a fastidious study rather than a cursory and myopic approach to all the presented material can effectuate palpable divorce healing. While intentionally compact, this book is not designed to be an accelerated and leisurely read. It is intentionally concise, and inexpensive, thereby designed as appealing to the limited emotional energy (focus) and financial resources of many divorce victims. Each reader is urged to consume and digest every morsel of the above material as though she/he were dining on a fine filet mignon. While this may seem excruciatingly hyperbolic it would be ludicrous to do otherwise and expect the genesis of substantive healing results.

Another enlightening rough analogy would be for me to expect to lose ten pounds of excess weight in only one brief trip to the gym. However, were I to devote time and daily perseverance to my weight loss goal it could readily be achieved. Those disoriented divorce victims who pursue only the cavalier approach are unfortunately doomed to failure. For in intimating self-healing by deriving self-solutions based on unsubstantiated information they place a psychic Band-Aid on a severe trauma. They are calculating a nebulous remedy by means of an errant algorithm.

This is dismally exemplified by the current metrics which indicate a 60 percent divorce rate in second marriages. Do not be fooled by the toxicity of lethargy. This terse aphorism is axiomatic for your genuine healing progress. If you are absolutely serious about healing from the tragedy of your unexpected divorce then compel yourself to conscientiously study and apply the proven recommendations, strategies, and *suggestions* contained within this volume. The dividends will be profound. As you resonate with the plethora of provocative concepts which you have been and will be encountering remain steadfast and remember that "the divine therapist" is always available for counsel.

Although you have been absorbing much information, a consequence for some delving into this affective and cognitive endeavor may become the persistence of an existential skepticism. This is certainly neither unusual nor unnatural. You have been severely hurt by the person that you most trusted in your life. You have confided your deepest thoughts and shared very tender moments with the one who has betrayed you. As a result of this duplicity your ability to trust has been shattered. If this disloyalty has been further exacerbated by sexual infidelity, the very core of your being has probably been lacerated. Consequently, while you ask, "Where am I going?" All of the above torment seems to converge within a vortex whirling endlessly around your inability to demonstrate trust and find direction. This deficiency in your current incapability to trust and reorient yourself seems to insidiously engulf everyone and everything. It liminally portends a state of depression. It may even appear virtually impossible to believe that you possess the capacity to heal from your divorce. Trusting in nothing may seem to be the only thing in which you can currently trust. This concept is further complicated by a retrograded sense of personal progression.

It is not an oversimplification to conclude that being enmeshed in the above situation is the result of the totality and frequency evidenced in a typically unreleased anger. Despite considerable effort, you may continue to be excessively agitated with all aspects of your life. In a posture of this magnitude, obviously the emergence of divorce healing is virtually overwhelming. If this is your current plight, do not think that you are engaging in the jargon of a mere "temper tantrum." Anger is a natural human emotion. Conversely, a massive anger, or fury, is a highly frenzied mania resembling a type of "temporary" insanity. At this immense level of anger, which is quite rare for the victim of divorce, perhaps professional psychotherapy needs to be sought. There are actual physical changes in the brain, which result from this very high degree of anger, referred to as rage.

However, most victims of divorce, experience assertive although normal amounts of anger which does not contain the constancy and depth of fury or rage. Yet if you are to progress in your divorce healing, frequent bouts with a normal unreleased anger must be tempered, controlled and ideally eliminated. You must realize that your anger, whether pent-up or actively demonstrated, is allowing your former spouse to control and dominate you. Additionally, it obfuscates the clarity of your thinking, thereby, debilitating your divorce healing progress. It also flies in the face of a rational conception of the spirituality, which will holistically permit your healthy healing. The opportunity to self-examine authentic methods of controlling your anger is a critical exercise prior to the internalization and implementation of any divorce healing strategies and *suggestions* provided in subsequent chapters.

A tenably working definition of anger from the perspective of divorce healing is now warranted. Holding a negative position, anger particularly for the victim of an unforeseen divorce, is arguably one of the most potent of human emotions. It is an intensely aggressive state of mind aroused by the response to being deeply mistreated. The tendency toward unmitigated anger is the privation of rational composure which can be conducive toward a demonstrable unhealthy dominance over other human cognitive functions. It vitiates trust. It obfuscates logical thinking. As a result, some divorce victims do "lose their cool" or desire physical reprisals or strategize revenge. In general, this paradigm is uncivilized and not characteristic human behavior.

Within the purview of unreleased anger we can seemingly morph from rational human persons into entities with mere instinctual animalistic tendencies. The most pronounced by-products of anger for the victim of an unforeseen divorce are elucidated in the following subcategories of emotion. These consist of, but are not limited to the following "feelings": agony, confusion, emotional distress, frustration, jealousy, revenge, suffering, and torment. As the reader may speculate confronting all these intense sentiments facilitates loss of controlled direction and encourages mistrust. While the above statement is tautological (a needless repetition) for the victim of divorce, it is critical to comprehend that without augmented support one can readily become bewildered to the point of despondency.

Another penetrating caveat to profoundly consider relative to the above is the following: you will subvert any healthy developmental progress if adherence to anger impels the "*schadenfreude* effect." This effect is extremely common to the excessively angered and effusive divorced victim. Essentially, the "*schadenfreude* effect," for this consideration, is the peculiar desire to take pleasure in any misfortune of your former spouse. This impetus is a clear example of the rendering obsequious control to your former spouse. It demonstrates itself in the futile hope that, in some bizarre fashion, the victim of divorce is somehow causing pain to her or his former spouse. However, the reality is a continued toxicity of said victim's divorce healing progress. The veracity of this ineffective mental technique is non-existent. It is a feeble and vacuous enterprise which when quashed demonstrates healthy healing progress. *If* it is allowed to metastasize *then* the resulting effect is caustic to the already angered victim. This "if…then" proposition will have deleterious effects on one's divorce healing process. The reader can readily observe the variety of specious facades, which a radical anger may assume.

In addition to the above assertions, one who has a sincere inclination toward healing from an unexpected divorce must drill down into another inconvenient truth. This is "The Paradox of Anger and Despondency." The previous paragraphs have elucidated some informative ideas concerning the emotion of anger. Now it is significant to grasp a focused understanding of the feeling of despondency. The two potent emotional attitudes are correlative in a subtly paradoxical manner. This is particularly the ad hoc case for one determined to heal from the anguish an unexpected divorce.

For our purposes, the "despondent" is a woman or man who currently feels hopelessly discouraged by being trapped in the abyss of her or his previous divorce. In colloquial terms, we may say that this individual is "broken-hearted." She or he is seemingly devastated by a forlorn spirit of dejection while maintaining a depressive attitude. Hence, the despondent is disheartened, grief-stricken, and prone to despair.

This "paradox," as viewed through the above lens, is a type of contradiction which contains some miniscule degree of truth. In divorce healing terms, the paradox is a simultaneous *co-existence* of both anger and despondency which *co-function* within their victim. Both feelings contain the aforementioned emotional by-products and both contribute to a state of mistrust and lack of direction. The reader can normally comprehend this paradox as being plausible since virtually all victims of an unforeseen divorce experience both these feelings of anger and despondency concurrently.

A stifling lack of trust also becomes a hauntingly quotidian reality. It is contingent upon your specific personality and individual disposition as to which emotion is initially or more demonstrably felt. Yet this contingency matters little since both anger and despondency appear to occur with instantaneous simultaneity. Essentially, what is being *suggested* is that your divorce has provoked such an enormous amount of uncontrolled hurt, unadulterated anger, and unbridled mistrust that it becomes virtually impossible to decipher a direction to escape the labyrinth in which you now subsist.

Concisely expressed, "The Paradox of Anger and Despondency" asserts that one's anger controls the victim of divorce with such a dismal energy that it actually hurts the angered individual more than it aggrieves the anticipated agent. This intended hurt of the other (God, the former spouse, the universe) "backfires" to hurt only the angered victim. In similar fashion, the feeling of despondency elicits additional anger as a result of one's personal anguish or depressive attitude. The cyclic nature of the "paradox" virtually consumes the victim. This occurs to the degree that the despondency inflates one's anger, ironically, toward the despondent whose personal lack of self-control is further surrendered to a specific dominating other—e.g., God, the former spouse, the entire universe. Neither the anger nor the despondency produce the intended results, in point of fact, just the opposite situation emanates. The entire attempt is specious.

Based upon my personal unanticipated and undeserved divorce experiences, and with the reader's permission, I will attempt to illustrate the above paradox. With a staunch anger, I thought that certain deliberately tailored efforts would inflict psychic pain on my former spouse. While in reality I was actually and more profoundly only debilitating myself. Consequently, in the throes of an obfuscated condition this miscalculation had relegated control of my anger to the other. A precise reversal of my intention had transpired. In my despondency, I presumed that emotional relief would come from the anger emitted at the other for deeply offending me. However, it became a cyclic paradox in which the more I hurt the angrier I became and the angrier I became the more I continued to hurt only myself. It took me quite a while to realize just how much this exercise in futility was vitiating my divorce healing progress. This virulent notion engaged a highly precipitous area. It is hoped that my foolhardy endeavor will be a profitable teaching moment for every angered and despondent victim of an unanticipated divorce.

Unlike the fact that a recovered member of AA is always an alcoholic, you will not be a victim ad infinitum. Your current objective is to be a healthy, healed survivor. In time and with the proper use of your holistic spirituality activated in candid communication with God, you will ultimately become a flourishing "thriver." Yet in common parlance, those divorce victims who aim at nothing, hit it 100 percent of the time. Therefore, do not victimize yourself but rather use all the material, resources and *suggestions* presented to you.

Currently, you may be exhausted but with the direction of the Holy Spirit, you will become indefatigable. Do not permit your anger and despondency to draw you into fallacious and irrationally injurious conclusions. Never capitulate to a learned and reinforced helplessness during the challenges of your divorce healing progression. Simply stated, do not waste precious time in an incoherent and feeble attempt to concoct your own divorce healing schema. Recall the tenor of this chapter purports the inherence of your holistic spirituality as healing activities (exercises) which neutralize divorce doldrums while interactively communicating with God for guidance. This is the only credible "technique," which conjoins the corporeal and the spiritual, the human with the divine, to advance you authentic unanticipated divorce healing progress.

As the reader can ascertain, the "*quo vadis*" question is propaedeutic since its preliminary interrogative direction impels the victim of an unanticipated divorce to move forward in arduous self-examination. For there is genuinely no possibility of a healthy divorce healing without the tempering (and eventual elimination) of anger, despondency and mistrust. Hence, with no sense of trepidation these feelings must be conclusively resolved. Ironically, while you may possess these debilitating emotions, encouragement will come in the knowledge that you also do contain the currency to abrogate their effects on your healing. Another rather obvious question now comes to fruition—how do I begin to accomplish this seemingly herculean task?

The aforementioned propaedeutic question which introduces a more profound study of the healthy divorce healing enterprise must engage the discourse. The answer is categorically bound to your attitude. The archaic axiom, "attitude is everything" is both vibrant and pertinent in this context. In terms of fallen human nature, there is really nothing new under the sun. Hence, recall the critical prerequisite need for self-examination regarding your personal persuasion toward anger and despondency. In so doing, there are necessary considerations which you are required to conscientiously address. You begin this undertaking by extrapolating from the following certitude. You were not responsible for your unanticipated divorce. This is a given, however, *you now hold complete responsibility for your present and future divorce healing.*

If you currently acknowledge this truism with tenacity, then you possess the necessary seminal attitude to move forward. Certainly, it would be ludicrous for you to be exuberant about the tragedy of your divorce. Yet you must gradually become aware that all of the anger and despondency contained in this expanding cosmos will not change a scintilla of the parameters characterizing your traumatic event. What is being *suggested* is that you are now obliged to conceive of your anger and despondency as absolutely useless endeavors in your divorce healing process. In fact, they are self-virulent and actively toxic to the appropriately lucid attitude for you to heal. The healthy attitude will ironically admit that the future will summarily demonstrate how this unforeseen divorce has provided you with a free new life. As was previously mentioned, by an unanticipated divorce healing veteran survivor in her own vernacular, "You dodged a bullet!"

The inductive (observable/empirical) data suggests that human anger and despondency can synthesize into an inexorably intractable alliance which is ultimately self-defeating. This conflated insidious entity is grounded and formed upon a tenuous foundation. What can readily be observed, especially by the victim of an unforeseen divorce, is that due to a laxity in self-discipline tenably defending a program of revenge directed to the former spouse emanates.

The evolution of this machination permits a cyclic inconsistency to occur. Not ironically, the victim fallaciously confident of becoming the victor ascertains that her/his ploy has gone awry and persists in only devastating the desired divorce healing progress. The victim has now initiated a new plague. The entire anger, despondency, revenge cycle has become akin to running an emotional treadmill, always returning to the locus of origin without ever advancing. It is an exercise in futility and self-duplicity. Simply stated, the provocateur of this anger, despondency, and revenge scenario only, "beats up her or himself." Finally, in an equally foolhardy dimension, this entire misconception fosters the perpetuation of a bizarre obeisance rendering personal self-control to the unaware former spouse.

Once the logical consequences of this critique have been thoroughly extrapolated and fully comprehended by the unanticipated divorce victim, its parochial approach conflated with incongruously non-existent results will eviscerate the above preposterous paradigm.

By affirming this line of reasoning, the reader will aptly grasp how a cynical attitude can stultify your healing progress. Cynicism is derived from purely selfish motives. This may have been a prime disposition of your former spouse when instigating the initial divorce proceedings. With your entire being, you must viscerally reject any selfish/cynical attitude toward, which you may still cling. Having personally experienced the emotional carnage that selfishness has wrought upon you and your family, this is a lethal attitude to be organically avoided.

The other destructive attitude, similar in nature to cynicism, yet somewhat nuanced is skepticism. The skeptic, for purposes of your divorce healing, is the woman or man who blatantly denies the validity of the material which you have been studying as being inauthentic or impugns its veracity. This attitude is pernicious because it is bereft of any rational systematic approach to replace holistic divorce healing. One may consider skepticism as an attitude which posits no substantive exposition of its tenets. Its pseudo-intellectual attempt is to deny probative data without providing a tenably alternative position. For the skeptic, denial is its *raison d'etre*. If you are rigorously holding fast to either cynicism or skepticism these manifestations should be very ephemeral as they are obstacles which will only impede your genuine divorce healing progress. Eliminate them post haste.

Hence, if you truly are absolutely dedicated and determined to heal from your unexpected divorce you must dispense with the negativity generated by anger, despondency and mistrust. Recall, that the herculean question persists, "How do I rid myself of these vitiating feelings?" A coherent response to this question segues to the propaedeutic, "*quo vadis*" question. Initiating strategic and stringent forethought is a prerequisite tactic in the design of a responsible answer. Inherently, forethought requires both appropriate structured silent time and systematic reflection.

Quo Vadis?

A considerable amount of the answer lies in your possession of the proper attitude. The reader will no doubt then ask, "How do I develop this proper attitude?" You must not assume a cavalier or reticent posture toward the aforementioned self-examination. Require yourself, throughout the healing process, to internalize in a most circumspect manner. This is not always comfortably accomplished. A profoundly sincere self-examination may be arduous and perhaps difficult to comprehend. For example, if I am really angry at an individual how can I trust that person? If I am despondent am I really capable of trusting the one who deeply hurt me? If the source of my anger and despondency resides within me how can I have clarity of thought? How am I able to trust anyone or anything and move forward unless I lose my unreleased anger and despondent attitude? These are provocative questions which will enable personal growth to ensue.

The reader should be advised that the above self-probing interrogation is intricate and may allow for the possibility of premature responses. Self-interrogation for the victim of divorce is not a matter of parsing out vague and ill-conceived observations. It is a rather contemplative exercise designed for you to meticulously and critically analyze your conduct and reactions to the trauma of an unforeseen divorce. It is often an exercise delving into your personal complexities. Although a positive mental attitude will abrogate delusions and fears that you may hold regarding the process. It is perfectly conceivable, and somewhat anticipated, that you will initially be errant in some of your nascent conclusions.

As with most issues that delve into the enigmatic tenderness of one's psyche there is no replacement for a determined effort. One must be neither personally disingenuous nor myopic in this essentially unpretentious analysis. Concoct no excuses for the unconscionable behavior of your former spouse.

The reader must compel herself/himself to avoid subsisting in the fallacy that your actions or personality encouraged the unanticipated divorce to evolve. In the divorce healing enterprise, there are no half-truths or a little anger or only moderate despondency. It is irrational, for the victim of an unexpected divorce, to be only somewhat angry or merely a tad despondent or vaguely trusting. In your self-examination, introspectively working through trial and error, you will realize that the feelings of anger, despondency or mistrust can only subsist in their *totality*. To think otherwise is akin to quips of "being a little bit pregnant" or "kind of honest" or "somewhat accurate." It is logically fallacious. Hence, you are not considering, at this level, some trite impressions about being merely upset or a simple sentimental faux pas or trivializing an impropriety. This defining moment of your life demands honest evaluation. You are working within the cognitive and affective domains to deeply confront the assassins of a proper attitude. Once this is profoundly comprehended then you can "deal" with your true and appropriate reactions to each of the above feelings. Do not be reticent in your endeavors.

We each learn and develop incrementally. Often, this author has learned much more through failure rather than success. All of the above commentary is written to *suggest* one critical directive. You must conscientiously and with the fullness of candor self-examine in order to attain a healthy self-understanding and move forward in the divorce healing process. This is neither labor for the meek nor endeavor for the vacillating.

The reader is asked to recognize that it is an absurd proposition to obscure your attitudinal disposition by a consideration of "time" as the conclusive healing method. Many victims of divorce do feel that all will be well in due time. Some believe that time is the great healer and contend that they have observed this as the elixir for others suffering the anguish of an unexpected divorce. More than a few have concluded that divorce healing is analogous to a physical injury and with time comes cure. Each of these errant positions may appear logical because they are initiated by those who have not made self-examination a priority. It should be patently clear that this preposterous thinking obscures the real benefit of time and impedes the divorce healing process.

Time alone will never heal the victim of divorce. Time is often considered a measurement of change or a finite duration of a conditioned reality. Time, for purposes of divorce healing, does not possess the power to heal. It is a philosophical/scientific conception which is virtually impossible to define. Time, like love, seems to be understood by all rational beings yet is verbally inexplicable outside of the scope of physics. It is true that time is the stuff of which our lives consist. However, in order for time to have a positive effect upon your anger or despondency, it must be prudently engaged in healthy experiences. In this sense time is a catalyst, an impetus, a period, a stimulus but not a cure. Hence, these healthy experiences coalesce and promote a genuine healing opportunity. You will discover them in critical self-examination and analysis. Recall, that herein subsists the genesis and crux of the holistic healing process proffered within the multiple *suggestions* throughout this concise handbook.

Time, which continues to aggregate during the duration of your life, can only be a healthy companion in this journey if filled with positive and healing experiences. Without your body, mind, and soul being directed by these experiences you will remain stymied within an inescapable abyss where nothing of a healing substance can disentangle itself. At this juncture, it will become quite natural for you to have cyclically reverted to being again entrenched in anger, despondency, and mistrust. To avoid this noxious conflation, simply do not waste another moment of your God-given earthly existence. Commit to this holistic healing system which will help provide the healthy life experiences necessary for a controlled and directed attitude. This is really the only logical strategy to dispose of the detriments of anger, despondency and mistrust. It is the only method to observe and know where you are going. For once you have candidly answered the "*quo vadis*" question, working holistically through your anger, despondency, and mistrust, the genesis of an unanticipated divorce healing looms large.

In an effort to systematically answer that additional perplexing question, "How do I rid myself of these impediments to my divorce healing?" The core of this question resides in the above mentioned necessity of your personal self-examination and consequent exercise of your actual bona fide attitude. The following guidelines will be useful in preventing your anger, despondency, and mistrust from metastasizing. They will require frequent praxis, which is reflective action. Hence, you will consider each of these emotional "over reactions" and then act upon your positive conclusions. It does not matter which human disposition tends to dominate your personality. If you are the type of person who is melancholy (holding a gloomy spirit) or sanguine (cheerful at heart) or phlegmatic (placid and calm) or choleric (having an angered spirit) these guidelines will be most helpful just as they have been to many other unanticipated divorce survivors and thrivers. Consequently, acclimate yourself to a substantive comprehension of the ensuing subsequent material through a penetrating self-introspection consonant with its premises.

Beginning with the canon of parsimony, frequently termed Ockham's razor, which for our purposes, contends that the best solution to a problem is usually found in the simplest and most refined answer. This will provide a highly poignant point of departure. Therefore, initiate your self-examination asking for the Wisdom of God (which is Christ our healing savior) to provide plainspoken guidance.

Then, focus solely on your anger, rhetorically asking why *it* has not yet healed you. Ask yourself, "does my anger really affect my former spouse or does it only impair my ability to heal?"

Next, solely focus on your despondency, rhetorically asking, why am I allowing some other person to control my attitude. Ask yourself, "Is living in the doldrums with a depressed attitude helping me to heal?"

Further, solely focus on your mistrust, rhetorically asking, do I trust myself enough to try to trust others. Ask yourself, "If I am naturally compelled to trust in multiple ways throughout each day, how is my lack of trust toward other people helping me to heal in a healthy manner?"

Having accomplished a thorough initial self-examination it is imperative that you now continue to logically progress while seeking supplemental direction. At this kairotic point (the opportune moment) you must rely on the inspiration provided by the Holy Spirit in conjunction with your holistic spirituality.

What is being implied here is that the simplest and most refined control mechanisms for the victim of an unexpected divorce, in reference to those above impediments, will come through your holistic spirituality. Recall, that holistic spiritually is a unique type of personal "montage" whereby body, mind, and

Quo Vadis?

soul are interconnected, comingled, and interrelated with the variant components and the Holy Spirit.

Further, recognize that since each Trinitarian member indwells within one another and is The One True God, the gift of your holistic spirituality provides the following: the unrestricted creative agency of God the Father, the healing passion and compassion of Jesus Christ (the God-Man), and the fostering therapeutic advocacy and counsel of the Holy Spirit. Your omnipotent, omniscient, omnipresent triune God is longing to guide and direct your divorce healing. However, in the course of your self-examination, you must petition God's loving, healing assistance. God will never impinge upon your free will to request or reject the explosion of healing power that awaits you. It is a dogmatic pronouncement that the tri-personal God comprehends your pain and plight through an unrestricted love and omniscience. You were not created to suffer from the tragedy of an unforeseen divorce. (Recall, this occurred as the selfish free choice of your former spouse). In fact, by the scourging of Christ you have already been healed. Your challenge is to prayerfully comprehend and faithfully accept this absolute doctrinal reality. Consequently, through the power of the Holy Spirit, who fosters the gift of your holistic spirituality, if you *ask* for healing and do not debilitate the process (through faithlessness or obstinacy) the ability to heal in a healthy holistic manner will be gradually received at *the* perfect time as determined by God's Will.

Quo Vadis?

Despite all of the above dogmatic realities, you may continue to be entangled within a web of belligerent, stringent, and pessimistic intractability. In the depths of your being you, in fact, crave healing from the anguish of an unanticipated divorce. Yet despite an exhaustive self-examination your anger refuses to subside. This is relatively common to those possessing said intractable disposition.

If this is your current status, it may appear that the only recourse which you possess is to focus a suppressed unrelenting anger at God. You rationalize your way through this quagmire of discontent by means of a fallacious extrapolation reminding yourself that God has control of all aspects of the entire universe. Consequently, you errantly conclude that God knowingly *devised* your divorce. It was God's malicious concoction and, therefore, God's mistake. Desperation can often camouflage logic. However, your desperation and anger may be so acute that you have reached the point of abhorrence toward or even the denial of God. This was the author's initially absurd perspective and was equally held by virtually all the other women and men whom he has interviewed. Like an unfinished puzzle, some pieces would just not seem to fit. The accusation of God as the responsible party in the occurrence of our divorces appeared to convey a type of demented solace. Do you really believe that God (who is Love) created you to suffer the afflictions of your unanticipated divorce?

Much of the above acrimony is/was an effect of the Original Sin. The sin of our *first* "homo-sapiens

sapiens" parents (a monogenism, a human genome, a mitochondrial type DNA referred to as "the Eve gene," and a "Y Adam chromosome"), perhaps, from as little as six thousand to approximately seventy thousand years ago was freely committed at some point but is contracted today by each human person. While Original sin is washed clean at our Baptism, the effects of this Adamic sin remain throughout our lives. These effects are not only concupiscent but also incline all humanity toward covert and overt sinful thoughts and behaviors.

Consequently, for the bewildered victim of an unanticipated and unexplained divorce, a human desire to associate evil behavior emanating from absolute Goodness Itself is a violation of the principle of non-contradiction and an impulsively foolhardy enterprise. Yet the human mind (when obfuscated) has the God-given freedom to roam even within the implausible and spurious. This aberrant conception elicits no anger from our unconditionally loving God and may be a therapeutic venting for the victim of divorce. Much more will follow on expressing one's need for this vengeful disposition latter in the chapter.

Moving forward, if you have been studying this book, but remain conflicted then its only current appeal may respectfully be made to your somewhat muddled and perplexed sense of the rational and responsible. By an apodictic approach, which is logically incontestable, the process of elimination may provide intelligible and conclusive assertions drawn for the "embittered reader" through the following declarations.

1. A negative and/or obdurate attitude will not heal you.
2. Time alone will not heal you.
3. Advice from various friends and relatives will not heal you.
4. Anger, despondency, and mistrust will not heal you.
5. Cynicism and skepticism will not heal you.
6. A capricious, cavalier, or lethargic attitude will not heal you.
7. An anemic self-examination will not heal you.
8. Your personality disposition will not heal you.
9. Your lack of self-direction will not heal you.
10. Your denial of God's existence will not heal you.
11. Aimless recreational activities (the gym, drugs, sex) will not heal you.
12. A petulant attitude will not heal you.

Given these twelve propositions, how will you heal from the anguish caused by your unanticipated divorce? If you merely vegetate and do nothing, absolutely nothing will be the only result. Consequently, what is your strategy? *Quo vadis?*

What is courteously being *suggested* to the "embittered reader" is that the simplest and most refined solution (the canon of parsimony) to your genuine divorce healing is found within the gift of holistic spirituality. This gift, which you possess, is your only reliable response to each of the above negations. Respectfully, at this inchoate moment of your divorce healing you are akin to a child who fears the darkness of her or his bedroom. This darkness plays havoc with your imagination and immobilizes clarity of thought. You may "see and think" things which are non-existent and non-problematic. However, with proper educative exposure and the determination to prevent an inert attitude, you can be vindicated from this apprehension. Your mental aberration mystifyingly fades and you eventually recognize that even in the darkness there is some light. Your mind's eye gradually becomes acclimated and unafraid. You begin to see more vividly in the dark.

Christ encourages each of us not to fear but rather trust in Him as the world's light. Christ gave sight to the blind because of His compassion on them and their faith in the power He possesses. Christ took on all of your fear and pain and sin by His passion and death on the cross to honor His Father's love for humanity. If you continually suffer from the pain of your unexpected divorce, join that specific suffering to the suffering of Christ's passion. He is the "divine physician" who heals if you possess merely a scintilla of faith in Him. Your holistic spirituality, a unified comprehensive integration of your body, mind, and soul is the interrelationship existing between you and the triune God. It is the only coherent answer to the question of where you are going in terms of the divorce healing process.

Whatever may be the current condition of your thinking, this chapter is about to proffer a critical opportunity. It is the appropriate time for *each reader* to engage in an intriguing yet somewhat acerbic prayer. It has been written specifically with you in mind. Be assured, while it may appear psalm-like this is a prayer unlike most others. It will allow you to vent any "residual" disdain toward God as well as your unexpected, undeserved divorce.

This prayer composed and used by the author, will allow you to boldly express your honest and potent emotions to God. Ultimately, you will seek God's healing. However, prior to your petitioning the triune God, you will spew forth the venomous emotional bile which has been accumulating in the core of your being since that unforeseen divorce. The reader should be advised that while this prayer is purgative, it is neither a panacea nor a mystically formulated invocation. Yet since the anguish of an unexpected divorce is ingredient to you, the benefit of the forthcoming prayer will demonstrate the genesis of your palpable metamorphosis.

Realize that our God, eternally omniscient, is intimately cognizant of your suffering. One result of God's impassible nature is that there is nothing you can candidly share, which will astonish or aggrieve "the Holy Omnipotent One." Christ, who has already taken on all sin and suffering, craves your personal healing much more than you know. The Holy

Spirit, "the divine therapist," deeply desires to *treat* your most robust disturbances. Therefore, with all the depth of emotion that you can muster, demand from God in no uncertain terms, to be heard and to move toward healing! You are now encouraged to steadfastly pray the following:

If you really exist and if all this information about my holistic spirituality is true then I want you to know that I am extremely angry at you! If you are really the God of unconditional love, how could you hurt me so deeply and devastate my family? I never deserved nor anticipated this catastrophe to be thrown into my life by you, the loving creator God! How dare you destroy not only my life but also the lives of those who truly love me! Your actions have broken my heart, yet you let others who should be divorced, continue in their uncomfortable marriages! If you really do exist, I demand to be healed from the anguish, confusion, and frustration of this unwarranted, unconscionable divorce! And I further demand that you heal me beginning right this moment! If you exist, and if you truly love me, send the Christ and the Holy Spirit into my life immediately to give me a sense of direction! If you exist and genuinely love me—and since I have run out of alternatives—don't toy with me any longer! If you are hearing my plea, act now to lift me from my anger, despondency and mistrust! I have waited and suffered long enough—if you are my God, then heal me now!

Quo Vadis?

Allow the potency of this prayer to immerse itself within the very core of your being. You have not just prayed for healing to some fabricated phantasm. You have "laid your cards on the table" before The Almighty, Unrestricted, Omnipotent, Infinitely Unconditionally, Loving God. You have vented your personal thoughts and feelings while actually and boldly demanding God to heal you immediately. The clay has commanded the potter. You are strongly encouraged to feel good about yourself at this very moment. Perhaps, this has been the very first time that you have honestly and prayerfully verbalized your true feelings. You have not used a pre-formatted or rote prayer structure but have communicated from your heart. These are the prayers that most assuredly are at the core of your spiritual nexus with God. Your anger and petition have already been accepted by God. Recognize that God is love.

You will gradually begin to heal from this unexpected divorce and its ramifications *if* you access the fullness of your holistic spirituality. Clearly, any divorce victim can question God's existence and verbalize aggravated intractable criticisms. However, this was not the rationale for your personal prayer. Reread this prayer frequently and you will gradually begin to observe that the God of all creation is creating a "newness" within you. You have neither threatened God nor stimulated God's ire. You have verbalized both your anguish with and dependency upon the unrestricted designer, creator, and sustainer of the universe. You have come before God in the candid communicative manner, which a truly open and loving parent desires of her or his child. You will never have a more caring and concerned lover.

As you continually reread your new prayer, it will become obvious that no pious platitudes were asserted. This is the manner in which each of your future prayers need be addressed to the Triune God. Prayer is communication with God. Human communication varies in its posture and is relative to life's circumstances. This human and divine prayerful interconnectivity of your holistic spirituality in sincere cooperation with the Trinity is absolutely no different. In order to heal properly you must specifically communicate with your physician what you are feeling and where you are hurting. As with all personal interaction communication is imperative. Perhaps, you unfortunately witnessed the erosion of communication in your divorce. However, "the Divine Physician" will never divorce you and is eager for any type of heartfelt communication. Appropriate your holistic spirituality *daily* to avoid divorcing yourself from the triune God. Recall, however, that prayer is communicative since its locus requires candid assertion and aggressive listening.

As referenced above, you should avail yourself of your new prayer as is deemed necessary through the anger, despondency, and mistrust which will frequent itself throughout the divorce healing process. However, it is not obligatory to restrict yourself solely to the exact verbiage. Many victims of an unexpected divorce may readily adjust the prayer to their specific needs or particular life situations. Use the prayer when your personal circumstances or emotions dictate. Consequently, it can be an ideal template for your own communicative creativity to be expressed directly to the Trinity. Essentially, what is being *suggested* here is that you do not ever stifle the obligatory interchange of ideas, feelings, and questions when communicating daily with your triune God.

Now the reader will assuredly apprehend the reality that earnest communication does not exist in a one-dimensional domain. For the realities studied in this chapter, you must communicate your concerns and any issues to God frequently each day. This is your quotidian obligation in the communicative process. God will also communicate to you. However, the reader may now ask, "How does God communicate with me?" God's communication is most frequently directed through the people, circumstances and "stuff" of your life.

For example, you may hear or overhear a statement made by a friend or colleague just in passing. Later, this statement may directly resonate with a self-reflective concern or one that you have possibly been sharing with God. The same is true of a situation or circumstance, which may seem rather common or perhaps appear quite startling, yet in some providential manner speaks to a personal introspective notion. Likewise, with what may be termed "the stuff" of your life (a song, a poem, a tender memory, an experience) in which you perceive a real yet inexplicable presence, providing some stimulating cognitive recollection or pleasant sensation. These modes in which God will communicate to you are unlimited because of God's unrestricted capabilities.

However, you must be mentally attuned by critically listening in order to ascertain a clear reception of God's communication. You may receive what appears to be a random occurrence of a focused thought (an insight) that for no apparent reason enters your mind. This may be much more than mere "daydreaming," depending upon the context, it could readily be God's communication to you. Sometimes, God will communicate in the silence of your day or the middle of the night. At other times God may choose a communication in the midst of your hectic, frenzied work environment. God's communication to you can be manifest in various manners and times. God communicates when and how and through whom God wills to communicate. There is no restriction in God's communication. However, your *aggressive listening* is integral to the synchronicity of the unexplained causes which allow for the "hearing or feeling" of God's communicative mentation.

Supernaturally, in the silence of your prayer or in the chaos interrupting quotidian events, God's communication is perpetual. The actual and continual self-communication of The Father is Jesus Christ, Himself. Your responsibility, especially in the divorce healing process, is to listen for and try to hear God through numerous experiences evident in other people, circumstances and the events of your daily life.

A contemplative study of the New Testament Gospels will also allow you to ponder the various pericopes which illustrate how God self-communicates through Christ. Through these various methods it becomes incumbent upon you to absorb God's communication and respond in a conversational mode. On these occasions, you have entered into genuine prayer. None of the above attestations is metaphoric hyperbole. This author has experienced God's communication countless times and in multiple manners.

Lest the reader consider the above as specious prattle allow, once again, a personal example.

Some years ago, while doing bench presses at a local gym, on the sixth of ten repetitions in my set, somehow, I lost control of the weight. Fortunately, a young man doing curls observed my plight and rushed over to spot me through the balance of the set. I will never forget his comment to me as we rested the bar. Almost remorsefully he stated, "I saw you kinda' strugglin' so I decided to help." I never again met that fellow but this was an example to me, not of fate, luck, chance or serendipity. It would possibly be disingenuous to consider him an angelic apparition or a type of supernatural entity. (Although, who can comprehend the methods, mind, and miracles of our God?) He was simply a young man just working out.

Yet I saw then, what I recall to you today, God's communication not just in the assistance rendered but much more in the young man's remark. "I saw you kinda'strugglin' so I decided to help." This is one illustration of God's communication and the message God sends to all victims of unexpected divorce. Occasionally, during the most ordinary or bizarre situations, perhaps through the voice of a total stranger, God shares the attribute of omniscience. God holds each of us in existence, is omnipotent and omnipresent to every person in any situation. Without God's infinitely ubiquitous sustainability every aspect of and each living being in this universe could not exist.

The ideal "takeaway" for the reader is to be vigilant in your aggressive listening because God ardently desires to heal you through variant communicative experiences. Especially during a time of need, synchronize your daily habitual prayer and holistic spirituality with the God who is ever present and desires a solid relationship with you. The dilemma for many victims of an unexpected divorce is that of becoming so preoccupied with solving their own concerns in a distracted and finite manner that they tune out the all-wise and divinely infinite solutions of the omniscient God. If you are determined to heal from your tragic divorce your holistic spirituality must exigently become the receptive nexus of God's loving and healing communicated directives.

As this chapter initiates its conclusion, admittedly you have been exposed to a considerable amount of relevant yet somewhat abstruse information. You have the God-given gift of freedom to choose whether or not it is beneficial to enhance your unanticipated, undeserved divorce healing. You hold a potent dual option. You can do nothing, using the infamous "wait and see" approach. Or you may opt to choose a proven strategic, gradually holistically healthy healing process.

You are fervently encouraged to judiciously review this chapter since some material may be opaque. Every serious student is keen on clarity of concepts as well as the questioning of presented material for more profound comprehension or disputation. It is a reasonable and understandable impulse for you, in this incipient state, to feel maligned by the unremitting after-effects of your unanticipated divorce. Consequently, it is to be expected and quite natural, for you to be a tad intractable and inclined to impugn some of this chapter's material. Further, you may be confronting the precariously dangerous temptation to improvise self-healing remedies of your own design.

Wherever your mind and heart are at this moment ask Christ and His Holy Spirit to direct you. If this is all that you are currently capable of doing, be assured that you are being focused in a healthy and healing direction toward unconditional, unrestricted Love. Your advocate, the Holy Spirit, is anxiously awaiting the slightest invocation to conjoin with your holistic spirituality. If this affirmation is acted upon you are in a healthy, holy, healing place. Do not parochialize the opportunity which awaits you. Also, when anger, confusion, and mistrust frustrate you to the point of spiritual recalcitrance either refer to the above prayer or simply create your own and then exercise your holistically spiritual components.

Quo Vadis?

The above paragraph implies that you may be to some degree experiencing the "zeitgeist effect." Zeitgeist, the spirit of the times, unfortunately is represented by a culture of death rather than a culture of life. The human free choice to corrupt morality through evil decisions has currently fostered a broken world. One effect of this corruption is the pseudo-existentialist position that humanity cannot discover an exit to our universal hopelessness. As you strive to heal from the adversity of your unanticipated divorce, you are simultaneously affected by the diversity of negativity which presently engulfs the world. Hence, a pessimistic attitude becomes the result of the contagion of this zeitgeist.

The reader must not permit the darkness of this diabolic despair to mitigate her or his staunch determination and capability to heal. In God's eternal present, God will rectify the world. Your authentic responsibility is to be single mindedly devoted solely toward healing from an unanticipated, unconscionable, undeserved, unsupported divorce. This chapter has provided multiple *suggestions* to move in that direction. The following chapter will be replete with various types of therapeutic holistic *suggestions* fixated on your divorce healing progress. At this juncture, you are endeavoring to find your direction toward divorce healing while being bombarded by a plethora of counterpoised repugnant world conditions. This "zeitgeist effect" not only promotes a culture of death but also exposes you to an ever-increasing belief that God is uninvolved in your world.

Quo Vadis?

Consider the following litany of negativity: abortion, decline in the belief of religious doctrine, escalating divorce rates, erosion of the family unit, euthanasia, global warming, homophobia, human trafficking, license in lieu of freedom, moral relativism, nuclear proliferation, political incorrectness, racism, secular humanism, terrorism, violent protests, xenophobia—contemporaneous exposure to a deranged world filled with these transgressions can absolutely affect your divorce healing attitude. While the ramifications of the above issues are global, you must remain singularly steadfast in the confrontation of your individualized personal anguish. Focus on the healing Holy Spirit rather than the destructive demonic spirit of this era. For each of us in the unanticipated divorce healing community, whether novice, veteran survivor, or thoroughly proliferating as healed, the triune God will be the only plausible and Truthful answer to our "*quo vadis*" question.

CHAPTER TWO

Suggestion Therapy

This chapter will provide practical divorce healing *suggestions* that have been therapeutic to many former victims of an unanticipated divorce. Of course, merely because a *suggestion* is practical in nature does not compel it to be requisitely useful in its scope. The reader, having completed a thorough self-analysis (the self-examination), should be prepared to freely and prudently select the appropriate and relevant *suggestion(s)* germane to her or his healing divorce healing process.

If you have given reasonable and responsible credence to the material provided in the previous chapter then incipient divorce healing is incrementally being initiated. Conversely, if cynicism and skepticism persist in the abrogation of prior assertions, this would not be an unexpected circumstance. Your definitive determination to heal in a healthy and genuinely non-acerbic fashion will trump any poignant conceptions (or misconceptions) that debilitate the imminence of divorce healing development.

Therefore, whatever may be your current attitudinal posture continue to study this concise book and introspectively deliberate upon its covert and overt *suggestions*. Each reader should unpack some reliability in a sober recollection of the old saw: you will miss one hundred percent of the shots not taken. Consider the value of heartfelt recommendations from healed veterans once traumatized by an unforeseen divorce. Many victims have arduously journeyed at length to ascertain that which is proffered to you in this chapter. You are already keenly aware of your self-obligatory commitment to utilize all ethical means available to progress in the unanticipated divorce healing process.

There will be nothing opaque about any of the upcoming *suggestions*. In fact, for some readers they may appear overtly absurd, obvious or simplistic. However, focus on the reality that often the absurd can be quite rational. The obvious can lack clarity. The simplistic may be unusually profound. Since all created mental or physical entities subsist within a sacramentality good concepts abound universally. The only real detriment to evidencing the good is holding an intractable attitude. One can stultify virtually any notion. It is very possible that you have experienced more than enough of this disposition during your former marriage(s). The parameters of your incipient divorce healing will be enlarged as you discern the reality that the Truth is omnipresent.

Perhaps, like many who anguish from an unanticipated divorce, you are so flummoxed that life appears to randomly drift into obscurity. Realize that today is the oldest that you have ever been and simultaneously today is the youngest that you ever will be. Hence, waste no more precious time pondering what you shall do? As stated previously, use this book as your point of departure. Study both its obvious and veiled *suggestions*. Glean creative or novel notions which will move you from the doldrums toward healthy and healing exercises. Why obliterate the stuff of your life by vegetating in the errant hope that divorce healing will create itself? When you do nothing, nothing is always the result.

Moving forward, it is paramount, prior to considering the delineated *suggestions* found later in this chapter, to meticulously clarify three possibly contentious areas. The first concern involves this book's use of the term "victim" of divorce. The second concern is the issue of the reference to "therapy" as mentioned throughout this work. Finally, a consideration of your blamelessness and lack of culpability for the divorce will be treated.

However, since this chapter is inextricably dedicated to providing you with practical real-world *suggestions* the reader needs be advised that each assertion must be intensely resolute. It is respectfully recommended that no offense be taken by its direct tenacity. The time for an inoffensive yet adamant approach has arrived. You cannot heal without a rigorous course of action. Therefore, while you will not be trolled neither will you be coddled.

Initially, it is absolutely obligatory for you to fully realize that you are responsible for your own unanticipated divorce healing. This must be your primary concern on the divorce healing docket. However, due to your God-given holistic spirituality, you possess the indefatigable advocacy of The Holy Spirit. Therefore, immediately avail yourself of the direction of The Spirit. This is the only genuine recourse of action to conflate your anger, despondency and mistrust into a spiritual dependence upon the Wisdom of Christ. You can no longer be hesitant. Emancipate yourself from the untoward allure of enticing temptations by "the father of lies," the satanic force of evil which is the devil. When you are tempted to regress toward feeling like a "residual" or acting with excessive anger, despondency or mistrust, refocus your mind and realize that you have given these issues over to the Spirit of Christ. Be assured the devil not only exists but is devoted to encouraging your suffering so that you conclude that God is unconcerned. There is nothing that can be further from the truth. Now is the moment for you to believe and act for both God and your divorce healing are imminent. Hence, with these preliminary thoughts affirmed in your mind, it is the appropriate time to clarify the first of the above three potentially contentious issues.

The opening sentence of this concise volume and throughout its pages the terms "victim," "victim of divorce," and "divorced victim" have been expressed.

A systematic tractate on this terminology is beyond the scope of this book. However, due to the sensitivity of, and respect for each reader the term "victim" must be succinctly addressed. No person wants to be a victim. Certainly, few people want to be considered a victim. In fact, some readers may be offended by the implications of this adverse expression. Others may find the term repugnant because it awakens virulent memories. Consciousness of the importance of the above considerations is at the forefront of this work. For clarity of purpose, when any reference to the term has been or will be used it is never meant to be detrimental or derogatory. However, for both the reader and this author, the exposition of a victim of an unanticipated divorce is the following: a once happily married woman or man who unexpectedly and undeservedly suffers as a result of any or all of the injurious action (s) of aggression, deceit, infidelity and unexpected divorce which was initiated by her or his former spouse. This is the explanation of "victim" as used in this concise volume. Let the semanticists argue otherwise. Yet just as you have rejected the category of "residual," so also while both you and I have been victimized, it is unnecessary to act, live or think as a victim. The use of this term in no way reveals the nature of our personhood. As will be indicated in the following pages, acknowledgment of being victimized, when properly understood, can be healthful and progressive.

Consider and apply the following scenario to your personal conception of becoming a victim of divorce. There was a negative change of heart, a cognitive chemical imbalance, a potent lustful concupiscence, an overwhelming selfishness, a latent immaturity, an egotistical entitlement, a narcissistic predilection which evolved within your former spouse. Whatever may have been the prime motivation, it was overtly excessive and stunningly appetizing to her or his prurient fascinations. Lured by the reality of "the father of lies," the evil one enticed her or his passions with the seductive attraction of someone or something better in some way than you. When this temptation was diabolically coalesced with your former spouse's free choice of the will, erotic disposition and anemic self-discipline, evil was chosen over good. This is how you became the victim of well manipulated and satanically inspired unanticipated divorce.

The above is of limited consequence unless you are desirous of allowing yourself to act, believe and continue to live like a victim. Do not merely reject the term, reject its connotations. Your former spouse is more of a victim than you have been. She or he must continually live a life of guilt and selfishness always needing to conjure up a defense for her or his duplicity. These people are entangled within futile search for freedom where freedom cannot exist. The end will never justify the means. Guilt and selfishness are two pipers not easily paid and ever craving more currency. Your former spouse must wear the current façade until she or he must succumb to the next overwhelming temptation. The oppressor is now oppressed by a cyclic vortex of self-induced oppression. This is the "real victim" of the scheme.

Your divorce healing salvation comes in terms of God's gift of a holistic spirituality which interconnects the needy victim with the subsistent Victor. When you are tempted to fall prey to the depressive attitude of being a victim of divorce, reflect on and respond to the following: would the unconditionally loving Trinitarian God, who designed, created and sustains this entire expanding universe (from the smallest sub-atomic particles to the continuously inflating universe itself) out of absolutely pure, unselfish, unadulterated, unrestricted love—not truly desire to heal and help me to no longer live as a victim? Would this same loving Abba, Father (Daddy) send His Son to suffer, die and rise for my health and healing? Would His Son send The Holy Spirit to me as my true advocate, teacher, and therapist? Understand that you are no longer a slave to victimization (unless you freely so choose) but rather a child of God, your Father. Your brother is Jesus Christ, the God/Man. Your counselor is The Holy Spirit. Given the Truth and Reality itself of all the above, now, it is the opportune moment (the kairos) to clarify the second possibly contentious issue.

We begin a brief consideration of the term "therapy" as both used in this book and the title of this chapter. An initial caveat is vociferously mandated: if the reader, at any time, has the impulse to seek professional therapeutic assistance with no sense of hesitation act on this inclination. This author is not a therapist. The concept of *suggestion therapy* has ultimately been a personally successful experience for me. However, as stated in the previous chapter, professional therapeutic facilitation (especially by a Christian therapist), is never denigrated in this volume. I was providentially guided to a variety of helpful, healthful, divorce healing *suggestions* through the realization of my holistic spirituality. This spirituality is holistic in nature because it requires the physical, mental, and spiritual components of which it is comprised.

For the purposes of this book and its healing *suggestions*, therapy is a type of curative activity (or healing activities) which may counteract the obfuscating effects of mental distress initiated by an unanticipated divorce. It refuses to allow passivity on the part of the victim of a divorce. It is blunt to the extent of disallowing an unreleased anger to control one's mind. Simultaneously, it gives recognition to a healthy, normative, sacred anger to be released against diabolic and debilitating inclinations. Its orientation moves toward the diagnostic assumption that one has been deeply wounded by the pernicious event of an unexpected divorce.

This concept of *suggestion therapy* utilizes a heuristic notion of one's ability to attain self-knowledge by the combination of having the traumatic experience of an unforeseen divorce with a cogent analysis of self-discovery. All of this is positioned under the God-given holistic spirituality innate to all persons. The intent is to align the divorce victim's determination to heal with proffered *suggestions* of a holistic nature. Hence, the focus is on the nexus between the individual's spirituality and the omnipotent healing ability of the Trinitarian God. In summary, *suggestion therapy* is a holistic approach based on one's complete spirituality (*body, mind, and soul*) offering proven recommendations which if applied diligently can be therapeutic for the victim of an unanticipated divorce.

The following is an illustrative scenario which may be relatable to the reader and offer more clarity regarding the appropriate function of *suggestion therapy*.

I succumb to the useless temptation to drive past the home of my former spouse. I observe an uncommon car parked in the driveway. My mind rapidly focuses on reprisal. I decide to pull into the driveway and continually flash my bright lights hoping to annoy her or him. I expeditiously realize that this is a foolish and futile immaturely vitiating idea. Hence, I quickly give the entire situation over to the Holy Spirit before it escalates. Then, with divinely initiated prudence, I decide to reverse and drive off. I refocus my mind relaxing it within a healthy healing suggestion. On the drive back to my home, I enjoy a laugh at my ludicrous and foiled action. My study of suggestion therapy compels me to realize that this errant idea would serve no purpose other than giving control to my former spouse. This has been a healing exercise.

A conscientious analysis of the above representation will provide a practical example of the *suggestion therapy*, as proposed in this book.

It is now time to engage the third possibly contentious issue for one who has endured the anguish of an unanticipated divorce. This rather common concern gravitates toward the misconception of self-guilt in direct opposition to one's lack of responsibility for the divorce. There subsists in the perspective of many the errant need to blame themselves for the occurrence of their unanticipated divorce. They become self-accusatory and guilt-ridden. Their rather sanguine disposition enables a pervasive sense of culpability for said divorce. Generally, this is the personality type which placidly accepts, even desires, to be the responsible party in maintaining the household. They have acclimated themselves to a position of self-appropriation of tasks rather than logically parsing them out to colleagues or family. As a consequence of this trait, or some deeper clandestine cognitive issue (e.g., a fear of not being worthy of love unless it is earned through effort), an overarching sequence of responsibility persists in every venue. If, the reader has the proclivity to assume this fallacious lifestyle, meticulously examine the following treatment.

The misconception of this self-deprecating admonition engenders the statement: "I must have done something very wrong to impel my former spouse to initiate those unexpected divorce proceedings." Recall in the previous chapter that you were asked to examine yourself in an extremely conscientious manner. A similar self-examination is exigent in this third contentious area if you desire to heal in a healthy fashion.

Once again, the occasion arises, for this chapter to be respectfully direct and lovingly abrasive. One who is overburdened by the above misconception must be patently honest when speaking to the only indispensable question that will obliterate any self-deprecating concepts. This issue hinges on the following pivotal question. "Despite the normal and occasional concerns which every marriage will have, did I ever do anything so emotionally, physically or verbally heinous and continually harassing (or abusive) to provoke and require my former spouse to unexpectedly file for divorce?" Be quite venial with yourself when answering this critical question. Simply stated, if the answer is *no* and that will most likely be the case, then assuredly believe that your former spouse was the primary cause, condition and initiator of the divorce. You are not the responsible party and, consequently, should release yourself from any guilt.

If you become overly scrupulous in answering this telling question then a version of the law of contradiction must be advocated. For our divorce healing purposes and final clarification of this third possibly contentious issue relax in the following logic. The law of contradiction affirms that two (in this case, emotional) opposing assertions regarding the exact same subject cannot be valid in the same sense and at the same time. For example, you cannot exist and not exist simultaneously and contemporaneously. Another illustration of the law of contradiction, especially for those blaming God for their divorce, would assert: Only good comes from God, but my divorce is evil, I know it came from God. Or God brought my former spouse and I together in order to separate us. Another common contradiction: God created me from an infinite set of possibilities so that God could make me suffer. These are contradictory and impossible assertions. Another example germane to the conclusivity of the above question is your honest affirmation: I absolutely know that I gave all my care and love to my former spouse. Yet my former spouse divorced me because I did not give all my care and love to her or him. Or I truly gave all my care and love to my former spouse but did I truly give all my care and love to my former spouse? These types of irrational misconceptions employ the law of contradiction (and common sense). They inhere as impossible states of reality. Assuredly, they are simply contradictory ruminations. Their incredulous logic flies in the very face of reason. *The reader needs be absolutely clear, neither you nor God is responsible for your unanticipated divorce.* Release yourself from any blame. Your former spouse is the culprit. Culpability lies on their narcissistic attitudes and behaviors. You can rest assured of this fact because in some manner or mode your former spouse has communicated her or his errant rationale to justify the initiation of the unanticipated divorce.

Suggestion Therapy

Often, though, it may appear stressful, in order to effectuate the upcoming *suggestions*, keep focused on your intimate relationship with the omnipotent, omniscient unconditionally loving God who heals. "Exercise" (physically, intellectually, and prayerfully) each component of your holistic spirituality on a daily basis. The Trinitarian God will be your creative source to employ these *suggestions* as necessary in the gradual healing process. Recall that it is the grace (the God-given free gift and favor) of your holistic spirituality which promotes the nexus between you and "the divine physician." Contemplate this certainty: "the divine physician" is Christ, Himself, the God of miracles who spoke the universe into existence. He is The Holy Unrestricted One, who frees you from any form of divorce victimization. He is The Sacred Love, Himself, who is your omniscient omnipresent therapist. He is The God-Man, who has already taken on all of your pain and sin on His cross eliminating any guilt or responsibility for your divorce. This is the triune God who desires, by your faith and holistic exercises, to heal you.

Words cannot articulate or communicate just how infinitely and lovingly true the above affirmation is for one who laments her or his divorce. It is with the highest hope that the reader may fathom this truth. Your actions are determined by your thinking. Your responsibility is not to heal your "broken heart" but rather to collaborate with the Wisdom of God (Jesus Christ) in the mending of a "broken mind." God will direct you to the appropriate remedies needed in every divorce healing situation without impinging upon the free choice of your will. In this regard, your primary duty in the divorce healing enterprise is to ask for the Holy Spirit's guidance and then aggressively listen with an informed conscience as it is revealed. You will hear the voice of God echoing through and mediated within the coming *suggestions*.

The author takes absolutely no credit for any benefit the reader may attain from these *suggestions*, which were provided solely and completely by the mercy of God. Consequently, it is with a respectful confidence in my triune God that I was compelled (despite my faux pas) to entitle this chapter—*Suggestion Therapy*. The title speaks for itself yet the ideas are only beneficial if you choose to internalize and determinedly apply them to your life. In that sense they can be therapeutic. Hence, while I am not a therapist I have painfully journeyed in your shoes. I can empathize and sympathize with you. I have struggled to heal. I am certain that a cursory reading or a cavalier application of these *suggestions* will be of little value. Mitigate the extent of your anguish and curtail the duration of the healing process by an uncompromisingly dedicated pursuit. Therefore, if you are feeling overwhelmed, it is understandable. However, keep in mind that you are not engaging in doing "homework." Rather, you are absorbing yourself in your "lifework." Thus far you have never engaged in a more preeminent study. The time has come for you to commit yourself to this healing exercise in an assiduous and calculated manner. Compel

Suggestion Therapy

yourself to believe that you are further blessed in your self-study by acknowledging, in faith, God's supportive Wisdom (Jesus Christ). The aggregate of God's unconditional support, the utilization of your holistic spirituality, and a disciplined study of this book's healing *suggestions* is the indefectible formula which can generate divorce healing.

Note well that you have been personally selected from an infinite number of potential choices by the Creator of this entire expanding universe to possess a unique body, mind, and soul. Your holistic spirituality is the gift of conjoining these three components to freely move into a more intimate and interactive relationship with the omnipotent God. It is beyond human comprehension to know specifically why you and I were created. Yet dogmatic teaching assures each of us that we were not created to be rejected by the infinitely unconditionally loving God. God did not create automatons. Rather, you and I were created as human persons made in God's image. We were freely given our individually unique holistic spirituality to be in a constant communication with God.

Simply stated, you have the unrestricted omnipotence and omniscience of God to assist you in your divorce healing process! Do not be apathetic or cavalier in the acceptance and utilization of this prodigiously authentic reality. Therefore, prudent divorce healing must be a holistic enterprise. By allowing the fullness of your being to discern healthy choices it is logical that a quality healing will be enhanced. Within the next few paragraphs, you will be exposed to multiple *suggestions* regarding the judicious utilization of your body, mind, and soul in the divorce healing process. An unanticipated divorce is painful, and divorce healing requires serious effort. This is a terse aphorism designed to prepare your consciousness for the ensuing *suggestions*.

Despite the brevity of this concise volume, the reader has been most patient in awaiting the proven divorce healing *suggestions*. Moving forward, keep affixed to those physical, intellectual, and spiritual dimensions (including both positive and negative emotional reactions) which are controlled by your mind. If you acknowledge that, with the triune God's assistance, it is your responsibility to heal from this unanticipated and undeserved divorce then use all means at your disposal. Beginning with your holistic spirituality and evoking the Trinitarian God's direction for a laser focus on this divorce healing. Look to Christ, for without Him you and I can do nothing. He will steady your aplomb when you are tempted to forget to be still and know that He is God.

First Suggestion: *Upon arising and prior to your morning ablutions look into the bathroom mirror and forcefully state aloud the following: "I am a good person made in God's image — today my life will become healthier because of the healing choices that I will make. Jesus, I trust in you and I thank you!"*

Then go about the quotidian experiences of your day. Whether or not genuine opportunities present themselves, privately whisper this brief mantra to yourself frequently. Consider that repetition is the mother of learning. Allow this prayerful mantra to become habitual. Do not hesitate to put emotion into this potent acclamation. At appropriate intervals throughout the day draw from deep within your being as you self-verbalize. Most importantly, believe from the very sanctuary of your soul, that this proclamation is now your reality. As the day progresses, be attentive to situations or circumstances or people that will allow you to self-demonstrate any type of healthy healing choices. Observe and then act upon even the most simple of opportunities. Finally, positively reflect on the innate goodness which you possess. Then recall and take pride in a particular healing choice which you made during your day. Prior to sleep adjust and evoke your self-affirmation and quickly thank God for your holistic spirituality.

Suppose that at day's end the above *suggestion* appeared ineffective. Further assume that in some way you, the daily opportunities, or your psychic energy were anemic. Things simply did not materialize. Perhaps, you felt awkward about implementing this new *suggestion*. Perhaps, you did not aggressively focus on the situations, circumstances, or other people that came into your existential experience. Perhaps, the memory of your unanticipated divorce was exhausting and vitiating your endurance. Or perhaps some other life experiences simply repressed your desire to heal and you sustained a lapse in judgment. Perhaps, your children (if any) or evening events were overwhelming. The reader must understand that you are neither the first nor will be the last person to undergo these real-world eventualities and indiscretions. I cannot enumerate the amount of times that a judgmental error was enacted by me during the healing process. Like many others, I plummeted (sometimes quite deeply) on multiple occasions.

The fact is our human condition by its very nature limits perfection and allows frailty on many levels. This is especially true when one begins to alter issues of repetitive character traits. Yet you must remember that these *suggestions* are not meant to be military drills. Rather, they proffer your specific interior self-transformative objectives. This insists that you continue to be hyperconscious of a positive future. Do not dwell on or succumb to a past temporary misjudgment. Recall that you are always and everywhere in the unrestricted compassionate love of God. Therefore, have a colloquy with God. Sincerely ask God to give you both the insight and foresight to grow as a result of a given mishap. God's grace is sufficient to provide you the determination to forget the past and to move forward with strength. This originates as a result of your activated holistic spirituality which is the intimate daily nexus between you and the Creator. Do not troll yourself. Do not bother to beat yourself up. Jesus Christ, the God-Man, has already been beaten extensively for your sin and healing. Fully realize the meaning of this first *suggestion*. Even when you err you are still good and infinitely loved by the God who will use this omission, in some way, to your benefit. Hence, merely forgive yourself and continue to move forward into the next day. Take this errant experience as a personal teaching and learning moment.

The reader should also be advised that these occurrences may periodically (even frequently) manifest themselves. You and I are in a constant battle with the world, the flesh, and the devil. All of these realities sometimes seem to overwhelm us when least expected and counterpoise the best of our intentions.

Continually try to realize that God is ever present in all aspects of your life. Consistently repeat and reflect upon your mantra with profound belief. Really trust in Jesus, the Wisdom of God. Act with non-perturbed aplomb as you focus with poise on the entire scope and rationale of your divorce healing rather than lingering on one singular annoyance. If you comfortably comprehend all of the above, it is now the kairotic moment to consider and act upon your second *suggestion*.

This second *suggestion* is a serious attempt to relentlessly remind the reader of her or his God-given self-worth. Rejecting the personal notion of being a "residual" (see the prologue and chapter 1) is a critical function of the divorce healing process. God is omnipotent but God cannot, does not and would not create you as rubbish. If you have considered yourself to be the residual material left over by another as a result of an unexpected divorce, living one more hour in this lie is too much. Hence, the conflation of this second *suggestion* with the first is to enhance your God-given self-esteem. Ironically, one of the most efficacious ways to do this is found by selectively crafting a position whereby one aspires to appropriate self-possession. This means that the deeper you delve into the sanctuary of your being the more respect that you will have for yourself. Ironically, the more you give of yourself to others the more self-respect will be returned to you. There is absolutely no intent to be capricious in this your puissance.

Second Suggestion: *No matter the amount of difficulty, really try to do something positive for another person today.*

Recently, you have experienced an enormous amount of selfish behavior resulting from an unanticipated and undeserved divorce. Your daily unselfish actions to another, no matter how personally insignificant, will release the psychic "happiness quartet" of dopamine, endorphins, oxytocin, and serotonin. This is analogous to the resulting feelings of euphoria after a vigorous workout at the gym. One simply feels better about oneself. It is virtually axiomatic that by simply helping another you also help yourself in the healing process. Your perceptual field becomes incarnate with the exposition of true goodness. This is a goodness which only you possess both through your actions and God's graciousness. With this *suggestion* "you are getting into yourself by getting out of yourself." As a condition of your human freedom, when you choose to assist another, you innately create a self-satisfaction. Know that the initial stages of your divorce healing mandate the personal discovery of appropriately gratifying behaviors. The magnitude of these behaviors is irrelevant yet their frequency is critical. The intent here is the awareness of being simultaneously both the doer and the ultimate receiver of any non-coerced good act.

You will progress in both self-respect and divorce healing by a brief nightly reflection of your holistic spirituality. Meditatively you succinctly internalize the reality of utilizing your physical, mental, and soulful components conjoining together to help another human being. To recapitulate, if you are a woman or man once victimized by an unexpected divorce, this *suggestion* advocates for a conciliatory view of yourself as created by the absolutely perfect unconditionally loving God.

Third Suggestion: *Only you can choose to progress or regress in the divorce healing process*. Your life is not designed to be static. You live life in successive moments. Yet all physical entities atrophy, degenerate, and waste away. You and I gradually age. The reverse is never the case. Physical reality tends to move in one direction. Your personal history is irreversible. You cannot regress in time. The historically conditioned situations which occur in time are unidirectional. However, you can reverse the effects of detrimental events on your life. Those events are non-physical realities which do not possess matter, mass, volume or weight. Yet they exist as real experiences and authentic episodes (e.g., your anguish resulting from divorce).

Engaging these reversible, nonphysical, emotional, cognitive manifestations is precipitous. In your divorce healing process, this reversibility is contingent upon their non-physicality and the reversing agency of the omnipotent triune God. Your self-responsibility is the daunting decision either to progress and heal any negative remnants of the divorce through holistic spirituality. Or to choose a fallacious "progression into a regression" (an obvious contradiction) dwelling on past debilitating emotional recollections, utilizing no spirituality, thereby, substantially remaining gridlocked in a bizarre non-static yet nonfluid existence. Recall, nothing does nothing, it cannot do something. However, in this nebulous venue, if you choose to do nothing, be assured of a negative deviation even from your current flaccid position. Hence, an errant decision of this later type leaves one lost within an incomprehensible state of progress toward regression, a counterintuitive non-act in the determined divorce healing process.

The aforementioned "reversing agency" in the above considerations is the introduction of the triune God. As a result of the non-physicality of your emotions and the loving omnipotence of God you have the freedom to reverse the effect of past negativities. You can choose to make healthy, divorce healing decisions that will elicit progress. Consequently, the acrimony, anger, anguish, confusion, despondency, frustration, and mistrust resulting from your unexpected, undeserved divorce can be reversed. You have the potential for divorce healing. However, all is contingent upon the confluence of your holistic spirituality being actualized in an active relationship with the omnipotent triune God. The all-powerful, unrestricted, unconditioned triune God can affect a reversal of your current distress. Your responsibility is to ask for divorce healing direction, believe with profound faith that it is being provided and follow through with healthy, healing, holistically spiritual activities (exercises).

It would be neither disingenuous nor ludicrous for you to hold a conception that indicates the possibility of an immediate radical reversal. However, because of the effects of Original sin, it is quite normative for genuine healing to occur over a period of time filled with holistically spiritual activities. Your healing is contingent upon the depth of your holistic spirituality. Your faithful attitude, actions and prudent decisions will determine the length of the divorce healing process. (Much more on this area of concern will be treated in the following chapter.) Yet ironically, if you are truly embracing the infinite healing power of the Trinity by fully utilizing your holistic spirituality, nothing (other than creating evil or contradictory events) is impossible for God. Never marginalize God's infinite love for you by parochializing God's ability and desire to heal.

It is beyond all human comprehension. Since God exists only in an "eternal present" He acquiesces to and inheres within no human time line. You may be shocked by the realization that your divorce healing has already been accomplished. In fact, you have already received the necessary healing from the torment of your divorce. This has come to fruition as the result of Christ's superabundant acceptance of all sin and suffering by His freely chosen death on the cross. He has reversed that which appeared irreversible. Your unanticipated divorce was nailed to Christ's cross approximately two thousand years ago!

Lest all of the above appear absurd, illogical and excessively pious, the incipience of your divorce healing may evoke a certain level of skepticism. The natural reaction by the reader may be somewhat apoplectic. "If I am already healed then why do I not feel healed?" This question is both quite expected and relatively common. In a finite manner, all humanity experiences the finitude of our world in terms of temporality. For our immutable God the finite past and future are non-existent. In the immanent Trinity (the Godhead) only the timelessness of an eternal present exists. God's mentation is incomprehensible within the finite human conception and transcends time as perceived in our restricted purview. These are abstruse theological doctrines beyond the scope of this book. However, God's desire is for each human person to exist in a glorified body within an eternal "joy" experiencing and envisioning The Holy Trinity.

This should be humanity's ultimate goal. The penultimate, for purposes of this book in "our" world, is a healthy holistic spiritual progress toward divorce healing. Hence, in your current life situation, please do not disregard the initial comments of this third *suggestion*. The non-physical, potently emotional aspects of your divorce can be reversed by the coalescence of your activated holistic spirituality with the omnipotence of the triune God.

Recall, that your formidable responsibility, is to ask, believe and follow through in the divorce healing process. This must morph into a habitual quotidian activity. The divorce healing has indeed occurred but you must actualize it with the fullness of your exercised holistic spirituality. If the reader will excuse the following very rough analogy at this author's risk of sacrilege: you must actually, physically and determinedly use your ATM if you desire cash in your wallet. The cash awaits you. It has already been deposited but requires your PIN to access the required amount. You and the ATM are inextricably linked. Given this crude but pertinent illustrative hyperbolic metaphor, acknowledgment of God's assistance conjoined with your holistic spirituality is the only realistic hope that exists for true divorce healing progression.

The reader's attitude toward all of this third *suggestion's* assertions can either be an existential threat or benefit to your holistic healing process. Relax and incrementally absorb the critical momentum evolving within you during the analysis and internalization of this *suggestion*. Pedagogically, the quality of learning is often directly proportional to the imparted effort. Since you are both the teacher and the student in your personal progression toward self-development healthy choices are mandated. These will provide both positive reinforcement for continued growth as well as a healthy and satisfying reflection at the day's end.

With the reader's permission, I will italicize a healthy healing illustration of real progress within a clarifying format. Consider the following scenario in relation to your third *suggestion*. This will be a typical reflective passage encouraging incremental growth.

"I made a wise and healthy decision during my lunch break today. Although tempted, I refused to send a scathing text message to my former spouse. Good for me! I know that I made a small but life altering choice. Perhaps this is no big deal for most people but for me it is huge. I proved to myself that I will not allow my former spouse to control me or my time. I am progressing. Tomorrow, despite the challenges which will come, I will be a bit healthier and stronger because of my wise choice in the divorce healing process of today."

Since your life is never static do not allow yourself to succumb to the diabolic inclinations (Satanic temptations) toward the incongruity of a divorce healing regression. However, as the above scenario establishes we progress in life's selfies rather than on life's silver screen. Take pride in the smallest positive progressions. Like most divorce victims (while the miraculous is always possible) you and I will most naturally heal in incremental segments. As you exercise your holistic spirituality with an informed and determined conscience you will gradually observe palpable improvement within yourself. This feeling will multiply because it is the result of your finite but determined efforts conjoined with God's infinitely abundant grace. Allow yourself to vibrantly progress in divorce healing and an intimate relationship with your triune God.

A word of clarification is warranted regarding the aforementioned abstract doctrine of God's existence in an "eternal present." This mystery is incomprehensible because of our intellectual finitude. However, despite extremely restricted conceptualization, dogmatic teaching fosters some liminal penetration. For the divorce victim, it is of the utmost importance, to believe that the Trinitarian God, who is unrestricted by human time (and in *any* manner) has already provided healing. Divorce healing will be made manifest in human temporality based on asking, believing and making holistically spiritually healthy healing choices on a daily basis in profound interconnectivity with God.

The triune God is immutable. Any change in God would demonstrate some manner of regression or progression which indicates a restricted nature. This contradiction violates the very essence, substance and being of the all-perfect God. The One God is three distinct but not separate divine persons. God is not a tritheism consisting of three unified gods but subsists as a monotheism of One God who is triune, tri-personal, three-fold, and perfect Trinitarian relationality.

Suggestion Therapy

The absolutely perfect relationship of the First, Second and Third divine persons who mutually indwell within one another is referred to as the immanent Trinity. This exact same (and only one Trinity) when acting within the world (creating, healing, answering petitions) is referred to as the economic Trinity. Again, there is only One God who is triune both immanently and economically.

In the finite human persuasion, each of us has a personal immanence (intellect, will, self-love) and an economy (management of our household necessities). In God, the economic Trinity is the immanent Trinity and vice versa. This is a central core mystery of the Christian faith. This One Trinitarian God subsists in an "eternal present" a timelessness, in which you are already healed from your unanticipated divorce. God's existence, unlike ours, is unrestricted by finite successive moments or human events. Hence, your divorce healing is not a temporal issue for God. It is a time related concern for you as you desire to "be healed."

The above treatment is a feeble synopsis of an acutely abstruse theological doctrine. However, for you as the victim of an unanticipated divorce, know that healing has already transpired—yet your responsibility is to accept and try to grasp this truth within finite human time by asking for healing, believing God has provided it, and then making prudent spiritually healing choices. Simply stated, your divorce healing has occurred in God's eternal present. However, it awaits your belief and the determined exercise of your holistic spirituality to fully come to fruition in the successive moments of human time.

A transparent examination of the *fourth suggestion* will now be elucidated. This *suggestion* may provide a myriad of concerns for the anxious victim of divorce. Consequently, its importance cannot be overrated. Do not be seduced by dismissive illusions as you consider its vital significance. The slope upon which you will trek here may be slippery. However, keeping an open heart and mind will allow the following *suggestion* to be translucent. *You alone are responsible for your personal dignity, self-worth and human authenticity. Your character and value must never again be defined or determined by another human person.* Consequently, if your previous lifestyle allowed others to control, define or determine your self-worth nevermore permit this vile and nefarious situation to occur.

It is not neurotic approach for any woman or man, victimized by an unanticipated divorce to become more guarded. Perhaps, you have very rapidly learned the defensive posture of acute vigilance through the God-given gift of your personal dignity and self-worth. There is no implication here of becoming an obnoxious maladjusted excessively nervous malcontent. While a respecter of others only you can be the responsible chaperon of yourself. However, like many divorce victims, currently you may feel the "I am so needy syndrome." Vulnerability is your plague. You have absorbed an inordinate amount of personal vilification. You are in need of your holistic spirituality more profoundly activating and developing under the guidance of the Holy Spirit.

Far too many divorce victims succumb to the rationalization of a precipitously abrupt relationship. Their thinking is that they will draw some self-meaning and avoid loneliness by searching for or dating a "gap-filler." This was the errant belief of the author (to the point of a second albeit brief marriage which ended in another unanticipated divorce). The truth is these casual dating situations normally end in disappointment and can be catastrophic to the divorce healing process. You will know when true divorce healing has occurred.

Do not equate coping with, recovery from, or recuperative measures taken, with genuine divorce healing. It cannot be advanced by the introduction of another attractive human person. Hence, never forsake your authenticity, as this is the genuine unique character which demonstrates the originality of precisely who you are in the context of being specifically human. You merely need to relax in the understanding that divorce healing is often more a marathon than a sprint. Divorce healing is contingent upon the depth of your spirituality's interconnectivity with "the Divine companion." This is especially axiomatic for the woman or man in the throes of an incipient divorce healing process.

While your intent may be innocent and innocuous, you do not know enough about your own emotional state, let alone that of your partner. This is because you are not yet healed. Note that genuine divorce healing is never the result of bringing a surrogate into your life. You cannot be defined by another human person no matter how potent their personality or physical attraction. "Arm candy" is never the solution to appropriate divorce healing. It is equally as irrational to arrange a date through another's personal recommendation, or by Facebook, phone, text, or website. Logic, prudence and God's Wisdom wail against this ignoble behavior. This is particularly true if you are trying to add meaning to your life by means of another person. It is an incongruous approach and a contradiction in terms. It is a violation of your authenticity and self-worth. You are in the process of the complete realization of your authenticity. You are within the initial period of a systematic divorce healing just unpacking the originality and the profundity within yourself.

I know these things well because my unanticipated divorce challenged the very essence of my manhood. Consequently, I thought dating and dining and dancing with a "companion" would help me find myself. In every case, the temporary pleasure eventually debilitated my healing process. I very often found myself back on page one of an unwritten divorce victim's manual. I obstinately impugned the obligatory and necessary time to healthfully heal. I thought that I knew what was best for me but I was not ready to be in complete possession of my authentic burgeoning self. Your end result may be quite similar to mine. Even though your companion may not have been ill chosen your timing and lack of proper healing can lead to toxicity.

This *suggestion* fully realizes that, with the best of intentions, both family and friends are encouraging you to heal. Yet often their recommendations represent typical pop psychology. Out of love, they try to support you with statements like: "get back on the horse" or "all work and no play" or "show your former spouse just what she or he is missing" or "revenge is the best medicine" or "it is time for you to get out there." These are the standard immature phrases which will further confuse you. Of course, it is obligatory for you to respect their desire for you to heal.

Perhaps, you have decided to adhere to their remarks and begin to date. You rationalize this decision because you are lonely and merely seek some good clean weekend adult conversation.

With absolutely no intended offense to the reader, let us agree that despite your maturity you are still a neophyte (as was this author) in the divorce healing process. This will pass in time with the proper use of your holistic spirituality. Understand that your selected "companion" may have absolutely no nefarious interests. Yet she or he may inadvertently be pernicious to your comprehensive divorce healing process. Follow this relational equation: two unhealed divorced persons do not equal one healthy relationship. It is highly probable that a given dated companion may be incapable of relating to your current growth cycle. She or he may not have progressed nor have the desire to progress with your firm determination.

The point is, that at this early stage of your divorce healing do not move too quickly even in casual dating. Scripture advises each of us to not let our hearts be troubled. Your personal divine physician is remedying you at the perfect rate. Nothing in the above *suggestion* is meant to be punitive or to keep you forever cloistered. Relax in the knowledge that you are healing every day due to your holistically exercised spiritual connection with Jesus Christ. He has provided you with your genuine authenticity, personal dignity and self-worth. You are made in God's image. Consequently, in the personal privacy of silent moments rejuvenate your growth and worth which can only come from the Trinity. In the holistic healing process discovered in this concise book you will soon be self-directed toward multiple convivial social opportunities. With continued attentive focus and trust, you will acknowledge some of these God-given situations in the forthcoming *suggestions.*

Yet this *suggestion* would be remiss in its obligation to all members of the unanticipated divorce community if it disregarded those currently involved in a serious and exclusive relationship. Again, I urge the reader to take no umbrage at the following thoughts. We have all entered into these relationships with hope for a better life. In each of my lectures and individual interviews, invariably at least one woman or man vehemently speaks to the "it's my life" syndrome. While I have respected that concept, I cannot accept its veracity. We did not create ourselves nor hold ourselves in existence. We are unable to ascertain our future. Our finitude is evident in all the endeavors of this life. Consequently, our lives do not really belong to us. Your life is a single individualized gift thought into existence by a mentative act of the triune God. From an infinite number of possibilities your life was conferred upon you by God's grace. You and I did absolutely nothing to deserve God's philanthropy. Consequently, it is a fallacious argument to hold that the life you have been given is your possession. However, it is valid to acknowledge God's gift of free will. Hence, we all possess the inherent freedom to make moral choices concerning this gift of our lives. You and I have the God-given gift of freedom to choose prudently or foolishly, to opt for good or evil behaviors.

Additionally, since we are created with a sentient proclivity, our physical bodies become the instruments of our corporeal actions. Our intellectual and soulful components are designed to aid the free and prudent decisions which keep us progressing in concentrated appropriate actions. Recall the holism found in Sacred Scripture which teaches that our bodies are the temple of The Holy Spirit, our minds are to be focused on the Wisdom of Christ, and our souls are made in the image and likeness of God.

If you are the victim of an unforeseen divorce and currently have a significant other, the above *suggestion* compels you to address some vital concerns.

You certainly need to cogently and candidly ask yourself the following questions. "Am I really healed from my previous marriage and healthy enough to engage in this current relationship?"

"Am I making concessions with my authenticity, dignity and self-worth as the result of a suppressed desperation?"

"Is my significant other possibly only a transition person?"

"Are we genuinely spiritually aligned?"

"What is the magnitude (the amount and depth) of our genuine feelings for each other?"

"Are we both close to the Eucharist?"

If you are engaging in sexual relations: "Do we both realize the complications and implications of this haunting pleasure?"

"Are there any idiosyncratic behaviors which I feel compelled to correct in this person?"

"Is she or he a person of observably high moral character?" Finally, if you have preteen or teenage children, "What is the honestly observable relationship between the children and my significant other?"

Assiduously delineate the above questions in private, prayerful and silent deliberation. The Holy Spirit will help you to adduce a personal and specific reasonably responsible conclusive alternative if necessary. In summary, genuine divorce healing (including your post-healing life) is never the expectation that your authenticity, dignity and self-worth can be provided by or ceded to another human person.

Fifth Suggestion: *Discipline yourself to become indifferent toward involvements or situations with your former spouse.* This *suggestion* is virtually an implied corollary to your previous *suggestion*. The genesis of it is ascertained by the reality that you no longer desire to be an obsequiously compliant servile person.

You are now reclaiming your authenticity, God-given dignity and self-worth. You must disdain the very idea of ever again being controlled by another human being. Through a conjoined efficacy of your holistic spirituality and full realization of a God-given self-esteem, the vicinity of divorce healing draws ever closer. I fully realize the demands of this *suggestion*. Generally, its tendency is to be the most formidable of the lot. Conversely, it is often the most personally rewarding. Regardless of this assertion, at this moment, the requisite enhanced effort needed for additional discipline may appear simply overwhelming to you. Even more problematic may be the anxiety caused by the notion of direct or indirect involvement with your former spouse. This anxiety, while quite normal, is enhanced by the fact that divorce healing progress is actually demonstrated by maintaining an attitude of *indifference* when being in her or his presence. However, in the progressive movement toward these objectives you will actually and pleasantly observe yourself healing from the divorce.

Herein lays the value of your endeavor. You will feel proud of yourself. This is most plausible because of the appropriate satisfaction that you will experience. Unmistakably an event of this magnitude is Herculean and yet you will have achieved it one situation (or involvement) at a time. An appropriate analogy might be found in your lumbering to the gym for a vigorous workout. You may not like the exercise but you will enjoy the results.

Consider the following: unless your former spouse is deceased, there is sufficient calculus to allow for the realistic possibility of a future encounter(s) with her or him. Consequently, for authentic divorce healing to advance preparation for this potential event is compulsory. There is absolutely nothing spurious about this imperative. For should the occasion arise, you need to have rehearsed your role. This requires a savvy grasp of several factors. Allow this *subset of the fifth suggestion* to manifest each prerequisite in a delineated format.

First, you must remain stringent in your determination to heal from the tragedy of your unanticipated divorce. *Second*, you must vividly remember the person responsible for your undeserved divorce and its devastation. *Third*, recalibrate your old feelings and memories so that your posture does not weaken in an encounter. *Fourth*, the demonstration of an *indifferent attitude* is a succinct affirmation of your lack of interest and apathy regarding your former spouse. *Fifth*, to be indifferent you must act with *indifference*. *Sixth*, recognize the reality that *indifference* rather than hate is the opposite of love and involves substantially less psychic energy. *Seventh*, any unnecessary physical or verbal contact is disingenuous and potentially vitiates your divorce healing

Suggestion Therapy

progress. *Eighth*, limited interpersonal involvement demonstrates your dignified panache upon departing (or abbreviating) the situation or event. *Ninth*, show appropriate courtesy blended with self-confidence in dealing with others present at a given occasion or event. *Tenth*, in order to successfully maintain your composure and aplomb during an event of this nature you must frequently rehearse each of the above requirements. You posture a professional athlete; whose conditioned muscle memory intuitively allows for quality performance in both expected and unexpected predicaments. These private verbal rehearsals will enhance your divorce healing. In oral practice, you will purge yourself of fabricating indiscreet and audacious remarks. You will prepare like an actor reviewing and memorizing the lines of a play. Yet this is not role-playing, it is the conditioning of your intellect in holistic divorce healing. Character and spirituality while non-palpable are revelatory. They illustrate your changing lifestyle and personal development in the presence of both the former spouse and others in attendance. The prudent choice of your words and actions becomes an astute indicator of your divorce healing progress. Additionally, you will notice that this progression is observed by others. It is a healthy feeling and a consciously inner pleasant experience that aids your divorce healing. You are demonstrating an authentic independence as well as a self-assured personality. Indubitably, with determined rehearsal and sincerity of attitude, you will flabbergast your former spouse and others present! Rehearsal alleviates the natural pressure of verbal stagnation during either a chance or planned meeting. *Eleventh*, no matter the brevity of an unexpected coincidence or a planned obligatory meeting with your former spouse recall that the Wisdom of God is *always* present to you. None of the above subset can possibly deter your holistic spirituality. Hence, a very brief invigorating prayer either prior to or in the midst of this uncomfortable exposure will facilitate your confidence in God's unrestricted providence (e.g., "Jesus, I trust in you.") This *Twelfth* and final requirement needs little explanation for *any* divorced persons. If you or your former spouse have children it would be the height of churlish behavior, deleterious to those children, and catastrophic to your healing where you to exploit them as pawns. You cannot control the boisterous or ignorant statements of your former spouse. However, you can control both your reaction to and rapid introspection of that despicable person with whom you now have become palpably *indifferent*. Should this detrimental experience occur, politely excuse yourself from the disturbing conversation and/or simply leave the event with dignity demonstrating love for the children.

To briefly recapitulate all of the above: it is exigent for your personal divorce healing to progress that you craft a sincere attitude of *complete indifference* toward any undertakings with your former spouse. This *indifferent attitude* is developed by frequent private verbally articulated and physical rehearsals (of varying scenarios) combined with the appropriate direction of your God-given holistic spirituality. Much more will follow on the necessity and value of holding an *indifferent position* toward your former spouse.

Sixth Suggestion: *Understand that your mind can only focus on one thought at a time.* Contemporary cognitive psychology suggests that the prefrontal cortex of the human brain is capable of sophisticated thinking and emotional stability. Additionally, our brain's limbic system is responsible for mood control as well as emotional memory. While our thoughts come instantaneously, the diverse components of our brain holds them in a kind of singular fashion. Perhaps, you and I may be productive at multitasking but we are not effective multi-thinkers. It appears that we focus and then refocus and then refocus at the "speed of thought." We are incapable of holding two thoughts simultaneously. However, we focus in immediate successive and constant thought patterns. This is akin to a-one-step-at-a time-yet-virtually incomprehensible instant method of our cognitive activity. You and I often take our God-given gift of thinking for granted. In fact, it appears that we are programmed to continuously be thinking one thought after the next. However, two or more thoughts never seem to occupy the exact same space at the exact same time in the exact same respect. Despite their incredible alacrity our thoughts exist at speeds in excess of nanoseconds.

Simply stated, the practical beauty of this *suggestion* in terms of divorce healing provides the knowledge that you can only focus on one thought at a time. Hence, when an unhealthy negative thought comes to fruition you can refocus your thinking and instantly transform it into a positive healthy healing thought. You genuinely possess the power to direct your own thinking. Consequently, your positive or negative thoughts are a product of your thinking. Recognize, as well, that the way you think reinforces your current personality. Logically, we can maintain that an alteration in your thinking will alter the thought upon which you had been thinking to a new and different thought. It would appear that a radical change of this nature is virtually impossible. Yet you and I are constantly in process of this mental activity. If we were not then we would seem to continue holding the same exact thought indefinitely.

As you read the above paragraph, no doubt several mental interruptions have occurred. Your mind has probably been frequently "jumping" from one thought to another. These distractions can be either external (a fire engine siren) or internal (a day-dream). Whichever is the case, your focus has been diverted by an impinging thought. This is not uncommon since the human attention span is necessarily limited. To some extent we can credit our ancestral cave dwellers with this interesting phenomenon. They were required to be attentive and alert in both self-protection and hunting skills. Otherwise, the result would be either the destruction or the starvation of the tribe.

Fortunately, by God's grace, you and I carry a similar DNA-like innate ability. The virtually incomprehensible speed of our thoughts often mitigates the likelihood of disaster. How else might we explain a young parent who while juggling several tasks is acutely aware of her or his toddler's every activity. In the world of academia, how is it that a student can "text" a friend and simultaneously follow the professor's lecture? How is a winning baseball coach able to concentrate on all aspects of the batter's swing while contemplating the exact moment to remove a floundering pitcher? The answer seems to somehow be inextricably linked to the quality of our rapidity to focus and then instantly refocus our thoughts. Yet despite these keen capabilities, we can only possess one thought at a time.

Herein lays this *suggestion's* divorce healing benefit. Inevitably negative and pessimistic thoughts will enter your continuous thinking. However, you are blessed with the competence to both halt and then instantly redirect your thinking into positive and optimistic domains. Recall that you can think of only one thought at a time. Yet the dimensions of your thinking will result in the length, depth, and breadth of your overall focus. Clearly, some people can retain a persistent level of deep or elongated or wider scoped focus than others. However, all of these people are able to project only one thought at a time. No matter your place in the above thinking spectrum, you can effectuate a healthy and healing focus. You displace the focus on toxic thoughts by intentionally readjusting your thinking and/or your cognitive environment. This refocus can be accomplished by your determination to utilize the three holistically spiritual divorce healing components (body, mind, and soul) to counteract negative thoughts.

Recall that a thorough conception of your holistic spirituality is understood to be a God-given organic relationship within the physical, mental, and soulful components of your being. This harmonious interconnection necessitates a dependent affinity with and upon the Holy Spirit. The somewhat complicated *sixth suggestion* is realistically promoting the notion that the components of your spirituality will aid your divorce healing focus. They will help change any unhealthy thinking by using a tri-fold methodology. This established method connects directly with your complete holistic spirituality by the use of prayer, physical exercise and intellectual stimulation.

Since repetition is the mother of learning, it is essential to reiterate the *suggested* axiom that you can only think of one thought at a time. Simply stated, when a melancholy (or negative) thought enters your mind, you cannot allow yourself to be stymied by lethargy. You absolutely must eradicate it through the immediate refocusing activities grounded in prayer, physical exercise and/or intellectual stimulation either conjoined or in any specific order yet coordinated with directed listening for the Holy Spirit.

Perhaps a realistic divorce healing anecdotal scenario will provide a more lucid and expository illustration.

It is 7:30 p.m. on Thursday night and you are preparing to watch a television sitcom which is quite humorous. You and your former spouse enjoyed watching this same program together every week. You are watching the TV program. However, your thinking is not focused on the comedy being presented. Rather, you are thinking about "those good old days." You are drifting into thoughts that are complicating your divorce healing focus. Although you genuinely try to concentrate on the humor somehow your thoughts continue to return to your previous life. Of course, you remind yourself this is now ancient history. Hence, you vigorously commit additional effort into focusing your thoughts on the healing process but to no avail. You are perturbed by the confusing confluence of thoughts emanating from the TV program, your old memories and the desire to heal from this unanticipated divorce. You can't seem to control your focus. You are becoming overwhelmed. What was intended to be a simple attempt to have some laughs on this evening has now become a mental conflict confounding your overall focus. You feel as though there are too many thoughts coming simultaneously. You become angry at yourself and frustrated with this situation. You have lost control of your focus. You have allowed a reasonably acceptable memory to dredge up old unhealthy thoughts.

How can you adapt the completeness of your holistic spirituality to resolve this particular situation? Immediately apply the following specific activities in an algorithmic sequence.

Step One: Without any hesitation dispense with what you are doing. Turn off the television quickly and put on some comfortable walking shoes. Grab the appropriate coat (if necessary) and hastily leave your residence for an invigorating one-half hour walk. This activity will begin the flow of endorphins. Don't be concerned about your appearance or the pace as this is "therapeutic walking." As you walk, think aloud about any subject that will alter that TV based melancholy experience (should walking be impractical do some other reasonably vigorous in home physical exercise).

Step Two: While walking (or any other physical exercise), move your arms and periodically rotate your neck and shoulders. Simultaneously, recite with sincerity brief inspirational thought changing prayers. For example, "Jesus, I trust in you." Or "I can do all things through Christ who gives me strength." Or "Lord, don't let my heart and mind be troubled."

Step Three: As you continue walking or exercising observe your environment. Refocus your focus by watching other people or concentrating on *anything* which alters that unwanted mental state.

You are extricating yourself from your doldrums by changing your focus. This is done by activating your intellect, examining the environment and enjoying your self-talk. You are using the fullness of your spirituality to take a negative situation and think it into a positive focus. This is a huge stride in your divorce healing. Recall that God permits evil to exist so that God can extract good from it. You and I cannot prevent the occurrence of evil in our lives. Yet we can allow our loving God the irrefutable opportunity to withdraw good from our evil thoughts and experiences.

This is one manner in which we partake of the very nature of God. The greatest method of this participation is your reception of the Eucharist. Receiving the true and real body, blood, soul and divinity of Christ will absolutely provide living strength and encouragement during your entire divorce healing process. The Eucharistic reception should top your list of weekly priorities. The identical thought is axiomatic for those Christians who, in a sacred manner, memorialize communion symbolically but realistically sense the presence of Christ.

Perhaps, the reader may counter the above three-step approach to focus modification with genuine logistical concerns. The following may be realistic issues confronted when one is trying to think one's self into a positive healthy format.

Concern: I have children.
Response: Either take them along or exercise within your home.

Concern: I hate to walk especially at night.
Response: Exercise in privacy and safety with weights or strenuous calisthenics.

Concern: This walking and talking and praying and examining, appears a tad creepy.
Response: Eventually it will appear quite normal and healthy give it a chance.

Yet if this is actually repulsive, discover any other positive thought altering activity and commit to it. Reading, writing, drawing, texting an old friend, studying a language, checking out Facebook, positive internet usage, listing future plans—anything healing and healthy that abates negative thinking.

Concern: I am physically challenged.
Response: Use your holistic spirituality to get fully creative. Allow the Holy Spirit to direct your refocused thinking. You will readily find an appropriately stimulating activity by utilizing your intellect to unpack a thought altering impulse.

All readers of this complex *suggestion* must realize that there exists a plethora of ways to alter your thinking and realign your focus. The God-given freedom that you possess, when appropriately combined with your holistic spirituality, is forceful and will elicit multiple ideas to create and activate divorce healing activities. The creative agency of God is infinite and your holistic spirituality is in a profound relationship with this triune God.

Understand, metaphorically you are striving to reposition your focus from the darkness of night to the clarity of daylight. Yet ironically, contemporary neurodiagnostic technology indicates that human growth occurs best during the night. Hence analogously, you grow when you are challenged by and conquer (even in miniscule ways) the dark nights of your thoughts. Dwelling within your holistic spirituality subsist a myriad of your own individually suggested changes in activity and location. This positive healthy thinking will morph into those virtuous habits which you will rely upon to resist negative thinking. Formulate a divinely inspired plan of intellectual or physical action by prayer.

During my divorce healing experience, I eventually developed the habit of brisk walking every week night from 10:00 to 10:30 p.m. While walking, I gradually came to the point of brief but heartfelt healing prayer to the God that I had earlier rejected. In addition to my walking and brief but inspirational praying I began to free my mind to think about a universe of ideas. Occasionally, I thought about deep philosophical concepts. Yet for the most part, I thought simply and pragmatically. Balancing my limited budget, upcoming bill payments, asking for a raise in pay, were all on my agenda and refocused negative thoughts. I thought and laughed about what my children had been into on that particular day. Frequently, at the end of this thought altering half-hour, I would explore new neighborhoods. Periodically, on weekend afternoons without my children, I walked, no matter the clemency of the weather, for hours. Ironically, I began to sleep more restfully. I share these personal experiences with the reader to simply illustrate how one can create a personal therapeutic walking habit. Clearly, I can recognize today the positive impact that this confluence was eliciting on my holistic divorce healing. God had been directing me to use the fullness of my holistic spirituality in a disciplined fashion to gradually heal. Yet if walking is not a feasible situation in your life, utilize the infinitely creative agency of the Holy Spirit to provide you with an alternatively fulfilling therapeutic activity.

A final consideration under the extensive scope of this *suggestion* may be the issue often referred to as a "panic attack." For those either unfamiliar with the term or unexposed to its ramifications allow a modest explanation. Contemporary cognitive behavioral psychology generically appears to outline a "panic attack" in the following manner. The occasion of a personally startling mental incident, which may provide incapacitating anxiety toward a given circumstance provoking intense emotional and/or physical trepidation, when no palpable threat actually exists.

The above definition is adapted from this author's personal experience. Some victims of an unexpected divorce never encounter this angst-filled event while for others it can be a relatively frequent occurrence.

As stated earlier, if one possesses the desire, money and time to engage a professional therapist it is encouraged. In point of fact depending upon the depth or recurrence of said "attacks" therapy may be obligatory. My personal experience with "panic attacks" was conclusively eliminated by a meticulous use of this *suggestion* and its immediate corollaries. However, early on, I felt that my entire manhood had been devastated. I knew my finances were virtually nonexistent. I was losing control of my very being. The loathsome feelings of claustrophobia and loss of family frequently plagued me. I periodically became anxious because I felt adrift. And yet, I was oddly but *providentially* being guided to begin a walking campaign. While somewhat unusual, this walking became my personal antidote counteracting each panic. It was an inexpensive and healthy remedy. It freed me from my lonely apartment. It released endorphins, provided physical exercise and never left me either bored or overwhelmed. This walking combined with brief sincere prayer and personally stimulating perspectives gradually alleviated the claustrophobic panicky feelings. I began to slowly feel in control of myself and this is counterintuitive toward the standard panic attack. I made walking a nightly ritual. My panic attacks subsided and eventually never reoccurred.

However, there were circumstances in which it was not physically possible to leave a situation and begin a healing walk. Yet the devil demanded his due and as a result I could readily find myself in the throes of a panic attack. Certainly, the refocusing of my mind was mandatory. Recall that God can permit the existence of evil to demonstrate the unexpected overarching power of the good. Hence, as a result of my financial ills, I most often deeply focused my mind on money. I called this mundane activity "pecuniary therapy." Perhaps, this concept will appear absurd to some readers but it was a blessing to me. I listed my debts, counted my wallet, calculated my paycheck, prepped myself to ask for a raise in salary. I focused on methods to increase my savings account. I did whatever was relatively appealing and personally important to refocus my mind and vitiate the panic mode. If this is your current situation you must do something similar in nature.

As previously stated, many of the divorced even while feeling victimized, never incur a "panic attack." Some do experience "anxiety attacks," which are brief periods of stress caused by an actual existing predicament which can temporarily disorient them.

This *suggestion's* overall recommendation for those occasionally stricken by "panic attacks" is the following:

1. Center your focus on God not on yourself. Commit to the reality that the omnipresent unconditional love of God is absolutely with you during any period of duress. If you apply your faith filled holistic spirituality to a negative feeling, God, not you, will diffuse the situation.
2. Refuse to convince yourself that a nonexistent anxiety really does exist. It is a contradiction. An issue cannot exist and not exist simultaneously. It is your personal cognitive creation. It is actually your mental construct bereft of reality. Therefore, in conjunction with God's omnipotence, you can deconstruct it by refocusing your thinking.
3. Ancient religious practices and current physiotherapy have taught us that physical remedies (e.g., inwardly focused deep breathing) will elicit a serene attitude. When exercises of this nature are performed in tandem with your holistic spirituality a God-given tranquility is evoked.
4. A profoundly determined belief in the potency of your holistic spirituality when directly activated toward an episode will negate panic producing thoughts. Focus on the reality that God has not given you a spirit of panic but rather of power and love and self-control. In most cases, that which we fear never transpires. Additionally, there is much truth to the old saw, when

we do the thing that we fear, that fear will disappear.
5. However, if substantive attempts to meticulously apply the above recommendations exhibit only limited results it may be prudent for you to consider the assistance of a quality Christian therapist.

A decision to avoid the divorce healing doldrums by simply attending a professional football game at a nearby stadium can help provide a realistic yet truncated comprehension of the profound interconnectivity within the holistic components of your spirituality. It is virtually impossible to properly accomplish this very manageable event without involving the "wholeness" of your being. Simply stated, the utilization of your body, mind, and soul is required in order to achieve this uncomplicated exploit. With the reader's patience, the ensuing football scenario will attempt to unpack your *seventh suggestion*.

In an abridged format this *suggestion* considers the following systematic analysis using the author as the non-heroic protagonist. A respectfully proffered word of caution: one cannot readily dissect the God-given gift of your holistic spirituality and yet the divine is present in the most mundane of human endeavors.

So I use my will to desire both escaping the divorce doldrums and to watch a good football game. I use my mind's intellect to determine the game time, travel time, expenses, and direction to the stadium. I use my emotions becoming excited to cheer a fine play, enjoy a brat, a beer, and get some fresh air. I use my soul's spiritual capacity to realize that since kick-off is Sunday at noon I must attend the Saturday night Mass. I use my body to walk to the nearby stadium. I use my mind's intellect and free will to select and pay the exact price for my choice of seating. I use the "wholeness" of my spirituality to sense the presence of God in the beauty of this simple but eventful experience while enjoyably walking home after the game. If this venture has served to alleviate some portion of my divorce healing pressures, it is another of God's unforeseen blessings experienced in a very human event.

If the above is an abbreviated version of the componential interconnectivity found in your holistic spirituality regarding attending a mere football game. Consider the complexity necessary for unanticipated divorce healing.

The seventh suggestion: *To stimulate the abundance of your holistic spirituality—physical, mental, and soulful exercises are required.* Recall that real unanticipated divorce healing resides within your holistic spiritually and its reciprocal relationship with the Trinity. This volume has introduced spirituality as the profoundly holistic interconnectivity of the human body, mind, and soul with one another and in union with the triune God. When this *suggestion* speaks of "the soul" the term is meant to include one's intellect (the capacity to think and acquire knowledge) as well as the human will and emotions animating that specific individual human person created with freedom in the image of God. When speaking of "the human mind," this *suggestion* is referring to the human agency that reasons, comprehends, formulates the soul's willful desires and enunciates its emotions. The "human body" is the human person's physicality.

If your impulse to heal from an undeserved and unexpected divorce is absolutely adamant, then despite any philosophically or theologically debated definitions or semantics, this *suggestion* requires movement from potency to activity by each interconnected component. Genuine divorce healing has the real opportunity to eventuate if you determinedly employ your spiritual components of body, mind, and soul as defined by this seventh *suggestion*.

Simply stated, you must utilize, by means of exerting various activities each of the componential ingredients of your holistic spirituality. Dormancy will not allow for healthy holistic divorce healing. The dormant condition is merely a prelude toward atrophy. Exercising the "whole" range, the holistic aggregate, of your spirituality moves your entire being toward divorce healing. The divorce victim exercises each component member to strengthen its efficacy in the complex process of healthy healing from an unanticipated and undeserved divorce. She or he is not trying to forget the past, but rather to learn from it. Divorce healing has little to do with acclimating, adapting, coping, forgetting, getting over, or a putting it all behind yourself. True divorce healing is about the God-given freedom to exercise self-control and empower yourself to gradually understand and continually develop the holistic spirituality comprised of your body, mind, and soul. This will only result as you study and exercise those components which are the essence of your very being.

Pragmatically, "the exercise" of your soul (intellect, will, emotions and freedom interconnected with and animated in the image of God) by means of communication with the Trinity (which is prayer) strengthens the divorce healing progress. Here, perhaps for the first time, you freely choose to think about, to desire and to emote relative to those issues of self-interest or self-concern. This "soulful" exercise activates and exerts your freedom of choice. You may decide to exercise your soul by prayers of adoration, forgiveness, petition, or thanksgiving. You are equally free to prayerfully verbalize any anger, confusion, frustration or mistrust being internalized toward the triune God. The communicative choice and the authentic activity flow from you. This apparently miniscule exercise has herculean ramifications in terms of the divorce healing process.

First, it allows you to communicate directly with God based on your personal mood at any given time. You can freely and candidly share a plethora of feelings. In blatant freedom and heartfelt honesty, you choose the attitude, the language and the mode while running the proverbial gamut of emotions in genuine communication with your unrestrictedly receptive God. Having expressed your concerns, interests or queries with full freedom and directly potent verbiage, you then relax in a safe space and with aggressive listening silently await God's forthcoming response(s).

Second, by enhancing your sincere communication with the omnipotent God, you exponentially increase your capability to communicate in truth and prudence to any other human person (especially your former spouse.) Your fear of direct and honest communication is abated for you have actually communicated with God. No longer will you "hold your tongue" in the face of healthy confrontation or avoid positive disputation. You can now say exactly what you mean and mean exactly what you say. Again, you have assertively and honestly communicated *with God*. Therefore, of whom or what shall you fear?

Third, your intellectual prowess becomes of little concern, since you have freely chosen to communicate (speak and listen) in poignant honesty. You will increase your own self-respect as you observe others taken aback by your healthy candor. This component of your holistic spirituality is not provided to craft adroit oratorical proficiency. You are communicating with honesty and freedom to the best of your ability. Hence, no matter with whom you are communicating, just get those first three words out and the rest will flow. Generally, the most profound concepts are best communicated in the simplest and most honest manner. For example, your best teacher was the one who thoughtfully simplified and honestly explained complex material. Recall, Ockham's razor.

It is the appropriate time to consider exercises that can enhance your holistic spirituality and move ever deeper into divorce healing through the components of body (physicality) and mind (the intellectual venue).

Thus far, in all your study and self-discipline, the reader is compelled to realize the axiomatic concept: that which is received is received according to the ability and attitude of the receiver. Simply stated, if you are determined to accept the material presented for divorce healing in this book and have applied your focused study, progress is inevitable.

If you (in your God-given freedom) have chosen to approach the general material and the specific *suggestions* as boring ineffectual pious platitudes positive results have a high probability of nonexistence. Recall, a university class which you may have deemed a tedious prerequisite or insipidly dull. Many students have experienced these connotations and either dropped the course or received a poor grade. They, as you, have the God-given freedom of choice.

The above commentary on one's potentially lethargic approach is respectfully shared with this *suggestion's* understanding that an inert attitude is symptomatic of a more formidable obstacle. This, of course, is not uncommon especially with the pressure induced by your unhealed divorce and the effort necessary to permit it to heal. The spate of emotions, which can be adduced at any given moment in the healing process, and the divorce healing process itself can be demoralizing.

If this is your current quandary, perhaps, it is exigently necessary to recalibrate the sliding scale of personal determination. If you absolutely and profoundly desire to heal from the anguish of that unanticipated divorce it can be achieved. Reread and really study the provided information. Relax in the omnipotence of the Holy Spirit. Review the presented material slowly and introspectively. Use all the God-given components of your holistic spirituality progressively. Recall, your personal divorce healing and this concise volume are never a sprint to some nebulous finish line. Healing can be attained yet often one must remain adamant in the diabolic campaign craftily inflicted by "the father of lies." Hence, understand the many and astute temptations to relinquish your initial determination, which "the evil one" will use to seduce you. Ingenious is the cunning of the demons that incite one to terminate an ambitious and healthy healing objective. Since your spiritual relationship with the triune God has been gradually evolving through the innate componential personal constitutive elements, "the forces of evil" are increasingly agitated. Aggressively seeking your Achilles heel, the Satanic one who futilely tempted Christ and to whom your former spouse did succumb, will not hesitate to alluringly diabolize any personal waffling. The devil's strategy impels some to errantly believe that the existence of Satan is a fool's myth. Be assured that apathy and despair are the bedfellows of the genuine unholy spiritual entity, which is the devil.

To counteract these very human proclivities for weakness, one must revisit the basic posture of establishing an ardent holistic spirituality, reclaiming the original divorce healing determined attitude, and following this volume's strategies and *suggestions*. Combining these counteractions with the well exercised components of your body, mind, and soul will mitigate any ill-conceived lethargy. Recall, that you began this course of study with a goal to be healed from an unanticipated, undeserved and unsupported divorce. However, the axiomatic caveat is: a goal without an exercised strategic plan is only a feeble wish.

Thus far this seventh *suggestion* has been directing itself to the "soulful" component of your holistic spirituality and its divorce healing exercises. Yet a full treatment of this determinative *suggestion* cannot obviate the interrelated componential elements of your body and mind. Considering the exercise of your interconnected intellectual and physical components, for certain divorced victims may be somewhat limited. Nonetheless, some type of reasonably vigorous activity will enhance their divorce healing process. In God's infinite Love and Wisdom, each human person has been intentionally created with the gift of dopamine, endorphins, oxytocin and serotonin. These are natural chemical elements released from your brain into the body to aggressively resist pain and elicit happiness. Concurrently, they can also elevate one's negative attitudes or pessimistic moods through physical exercise, intense laughter, satisfying sexual relations, and many other high spirited personal experiences. The intellectual and soulful euphoric and ecstatic episodes stimulated by "the arts" and contemplative prayer can also release these healthy disposition altering natural triggers. One ought to seriously consider the gift of this "happiness quartet" as another God-given grace in the divorce healing process.

The reader can once again observe with considerable clarity the virtual impossibility of dissecting and separating the component elements of holistic spirituality from one another. All work together for good under The Unconditional, Unrestricted, Absolute Love, which is God. In simultaneity, the convergent but never impinging interrelationship with this triune God is lovingly directing one's strategically guided divorce healing.

The reader may be reflecting on all of the above, yet, the obvious question emerges, "What are some of these spiritually stimulating intellectual and physical exercises?" Recall, the choices which you will freely make, while encouraged by the Holy Spirit (not mandated by your former spouse), are within the purview of *your* control. The reasonable and responsible absolute freedom to choose is now fully introduced into your divorce healing progress. This is a powerful declaration of your personal independence. It must now be exercised from potency to activity. Although the previous paragraph contains God-given happi-

Suggestion Therapy

ness releasing conventional experiences which aid introspection: the following is a short list of inherently more practical offerings. The reader should feel completely free to creatively personalize this docket in any additional and appropriate divorce healing manner. Recall, what is about to be considered has been configured not only as holistic exercise but also as uncomplicated recommended opportunities for you to freely craft your spiritual components toward divorce healing progress by confronting apathy.

1.) Choose material to read that will stimulate your intellect.
2.) Listen to the various types and styles of music.
3.) Write poetry or read the works of different poets.
4.) Visit your local art museum.
5.) Relax and enjoy a classic movie or television program.
6.) Visit a church, mosque or synagogue and observe the beautiful interiors.
7.) Walk and observe and think and pray.
8.) Work out at a "no pressure" gym or in your home.
9.) Receive the Eucharist every week.
10.) Spend as much time as possible with your children.
11.) Put more creative energy into your work.
12.) Plan for your future.
13.) Take a class at the local community college.

14.) Prayerfully read the New Testament.
15.) Reflect deeply upon God's involvement within your new life.
16.) Study a foreign language—perhaps, plan to visit that specific country.
17.) Take a hot bath in the dark and add a candle for extra relaxation.
18.) Savor one glass of a fine wine.
19.) Go swimming.
20.) Study a sunrise or sunset.
21.) Take in a sporting event—learn and enjoy the game.
22.) Attend an opera or a theatrical production.
23.) Learn to dance.
24.) Take a self-defense course.
25.) Get into a lake or river.
26.) Go to the movies—indulge in some popcorn and treats.
27.) Talk aloud to yourself or God about any issues.
28.) Take the occasional and guilt free nap.
29.) Appropriately make new and "real" friends.
30.) Try to live comfortably but simply—budget your money, time and quiet reflections.

The above thirty holistic prompts for your body, mind, and soul may initially appear rather prosaic or vapid. Recall that although they are recommendations, used by many others, you have the God-given freedom to craft more relevant opportunities for yourself. Their purpose, as proffered in this *suggestion* is three-fold.

First, you are offering yourself divorce healing occasions whereby, the experience of personal choices for enjoyment and freedom are exercised. This is pivotal as you progress in developing a new life with all its authentically self-possessive implications. The point here is especially relevant to that victimized woman or man who errantly yielded complete dominance of their self-control to an oppressive former spouse. You are using the three interconnected components of your holistic spirituality in reliance upon the guidance of the Holy Spirit to never again be oppressed by another human being. Now you alone are free to choose from a plethora of high spirited healthy activities. No longer do you exist for another human being's interests, desires or selfish motivations. Freedom of choice allows for freedom of life. You were not created to mollify the pleasures of some other human person. Recall the multiplicity of times throughout your former marriage that you acquiesced to the self-centered, ego-centric desires of the other, foolishly thinking that—this is love.

The second reason that the proffered activities are so vital to your divorce healing can be summarily treated. Notice that each of the above thirty offerings are a conglomerate of inexpensive, innocuous, sensible ventures (perhaps adventures) which will broaden you as a fresh new creature in Christ. There should rarely be a dull moment in divorce healing if you are seeking creative personally enjoyable notions from the God/Man. This *suggestion* is not referring to the *ennui*, experienced in daily tedium of insipid repetition found in those choosing lethargic living.

Christ, the designer, creator, and sustainer of this entire expanding universe is continuously encouraging you to benefit from the healthy experiences found in all His creation. You do this best by seeing that all of God's creation and all good activities in which you participate are essentially sacramental. Your holistic spirituality surrounds every quotidian experience because the Trinity is ubiquitous. As you progress in a faith filled divorce healing through holistic spirituality, everything (inclusive of apparent/temporary negativities) will work for your good! Hence, the above highly spirited activities, either found in this book or in your personal creative agency, are gradual yet substantial advances toward the divorce healing enterprise. In the scope of human eventualities, you are the product of your own choices.

The third rationale for utilizing the schema of the above endorphin releasing exercises is fundamental to your holistic divorce healing. For the victim of an unexpected divorce, a life bereft of healthy healing activity is merely a bland existence.

This apathetic type of divorce victim may frequently begin to devise cunning connivances to endure her or his way through the futility of an emaciated life. These diabolic machinations while intriguing to the eccentric victim are the result of an ill prepared and idle body, mind, and soul. Often initially promulgated by *schadenfreude* (the concept of deriving pleasure from another's misfortune) the bewildered divorce victim utilizes inappropriate measures in seeking information regarding her or his former spouse. These measures may include the catastrophe of interrogating the children (if any), family, friends or even remote acquaintances. Also included in this travesty may be the leaving of inane messages at the work place, bizarre texts or face book entries, variant degrees of harassment, stalking, and even the "coincidental" chance meeting. All these inappropriate activities are illustrative of the inactivated potential resulting from a non-acceptance of the tri-componential holistic spirituality conjoined with the Trinity.

Much of the above negativity can be deduced from an obstinate and lethargic dissipated divorce victim's lack of determination and an errant desire to self-remedy sans appropriate healing activities. This indolence can produce destructive, illegal, and non-healing experiences. When what is necessary should be a realistic motivational impetus for the sincerely determined victim of an unanticipated divorce. It is both counterintuitive and a *non-sequitur* to profess the genuine desire to heal from the anguish of an unexpected divorce and then be non-participative in your own healing process.

It is obvious to the cogent reader that this seventh *suggestion* requires meticulous study and praxis (reflective action). Recall the oft-mentioned recommendation to slowly reflect and introspect in the quietude of your day or night. A bustling life will still permit ten to fifteen minutes of silence. Find your personal placid locale, e.g., perhaps in your car or while on the treadmill or riding public transportation or after church or in a hot bath. There exist a plethora of choices and opportunities to increase your divorce healing progress while enhancing your holistic spirituality. Anticipate considerable dividends as you persevere by means of your efforts in conjunction with our gracious God.

Eighth Suggestion: *Stay close to the Holy Eucharist*. If you are absolutely determined to heal from your unanticipated divorce the necessity to fully exercise each of the three components of your holistic spirituality is mandatory. Recall, that each component is not only interconnected with one another but also directly reliant upon and interactive with the triune God. Simply stated, you are using the God-given gifts of body, mind, and soul conjoined with the Trinity to continually progress in the divorce healing enterprise.

For example, pursuing the system of parallelism, if one is seriously invested in a substantive physical exercise program then proper nutrition is an essential constituent. This combination of well-disciplined physical training and stringent dietary nutritive restrictions can result in abundant health and a resplendent physique. Analogously, since your holistic spirituality requires appropriate daily exercise, it also necessitates preeminent nutrition to healthfully nourish divorce healing encouragement and palpable results.

Enter the absolute necessity of the consummate spiritual subsistence contained in your virtuous reception of the Eucharist. Often both Catholic and many Protestant denominations generally refer to the Eucharist as the Holy Communion. This is the incredible gift of actual communication, participation in and union with the sinless Christ and sinful humanity. Catholic and most Protestant Christians vary somewhat in their understanding of the Eucharist. Catholics consider the elements of bread and wine to be transubstantiated by a validly ordained priest into the actual body, blood, soul, and divinity of the gloried Jesus Christ. The characteristics or "accidents" of the bread and wine remain however their substance, essence, nature, and being become the true and real Jesus Christ.

The general Protestant consideration of the Eucharist (Holy Communion) accepts the doctrine of transignification. Here, the symbolic nature of the bread and wine is celebrated as a spiritual sign of change. Whereby the bread and wine remain the same but memorialize the action of Christ at His Last Supper devoutly nourishing and unifying the apostles. This devotion and unification of the people of God is carried forward by the minister during Protestant church services to the present day. Hence, whether you are a Catholic or Protestant Christian, the potency and spiritual vitality of the Eucharist can never be fully comprehended or underestimated. It is the ultimate spiritual nourishment.

For the victim of an unanticipated divorce, following a valid and licit confession of past serious sins as necessary, the reception of the Eucharist is obligatory. The participation in the very nature of Christ fully present in the Eucharist strengthens one's spirituality exceedingly. From His unconditional and unrestricted love, Christ insisted on this physical action of feeding each of us with Himself to nourish/sustain our souls and allow every believer to partake in *the* divine nature. The victim of divorce can do nothing greater than to receive this supernatural offering of Christ, who is then present within you, as the perfect moment to candidly communicate with "your divine physician."

Consequently, as your holistic spirituality is being replenished by the God/Man, an incomprehensible opportunity of direct open and mutual communication (speaking and listening) with the Creator God is made manifest. In short, you are actually physically able to share any concerns with Christ while He is genuinely dwelling within your very being. Recall that each member of the Trinity is always present to you. However, in Eucharistic reception Christ is really physically present within your entire being.

A more perfect time to ask for divorce healing will never exist. Each of the more subtle and obvious *suggestions* proffered in this entire concise book humble themselves before the ultimate posture of this your eighth *suggestion*. If you were to do nothing else except impeccably devote yourself to a prayerful and sincerely communicative weekly reception of the Eucharist and live accordingly, the acknowledgment of being healed from that unanticipated divorce would occur. *Stay close to the Holy Eucharist.*

In closing this chapter, a very respectful meme of admonition is highly necessitated. If you consider yourself an agnostic or atheist, rationally and responsibly hold a conversation with a minister or priest to begin the process of recognizing the reality and veracity of the economic Trinity in your life. Doubting God's interconnectivity with your gift of holistic spirituality, enduring and substantive unanticipated divorce healing seems at best improbable.

CHAPTER THREE

How to Get Off the Couch

For many victims of an unanticipated divorce, the *suggestions* provided in this book and their individual travails often morph into an exhausting diatribe of what may appear as intrusively continuing recommendations and feebly frustrating endeavors to heal. Many do not seem to possess the sufficient physical and psychic energy to encounter the obligatory demands of a determined unanticipated divorce healing. Beyond question, genuine holistic divorce healing entails arduous effort conjoined with assiduous motivation. Since we all suffer from the effects of the Original sin, each of us can readily succumb to the demonic temptations of lethargy. The doldrums are seldom lenient in alluring an already exhausted personality toward the supine life. However, this errant impulse does absolutely nothing to encourage, foster or nurture the divorce healing process.

If this should happen to be your current experience, be assured that you are not alone. The inclination to "do nothing and hope for the best" is a potent subverting force and a façade for all those barely clinging to a desire to heal through the holistic divorce healing enterprise.

Physically and metaphorically, we must confront the lingering existential question, how do I get off the couch? More emphatically, how do I continually motivate myself throughout the complications that subsist within the divorce healing process? The balance of this determinative chapter will proffer practical *suggestions* to this urgent inquiry. The fundamental principle to exigently consider is the following: when the divorce doldrums suffuse, and they will, vegetating on your physical or metaphorical couch is not a refuge but an impediment to unanticipated divorce healing.

Nothing should be more motivating to you than a happy, healthy life healed from the anguish of your unanticipated and undeserved divorce. This is the postulate which should orient all of your actions. While a plethora of professional assistance by means of therapists, psychologists and spiritual directors is readily available, there is at least one caveat.

Only you, determinedly working in correlation with the triune God, will evoke absolutely true and comprehensive personal motivation. Despite the most acute efforts of thoroughly trained and highly skilled professionals, conclusively only you are able to motivate yourself. Only you have the God-given ability to thrust your body, mind and soul off "the couch." Since God is the first cause of all things (except evil) the requisite motivation to move toward healing activities is a condition of God's grace. You and I do not deserve nor can we ever earn this grace. It is a free an infinitely, unconditionally, unrestricted gift to each of us from the Trinitarian God. By its very nature God's grace presupposes a human nature which can thoroughly accept it. Further, whether or not one wishes to admit it our nature longs for this grace. Hence, God does use outside sources, including this material, as secondary causes which can promote a sense of direction and well-being. Recall that God also uses other people, various circumstances and situations as well as the "stuff of our lives." However, secondary causality is not the prime mover, the only first cause is the uncaused cause which designs, creates, and sustains all that ever has and will exist.

Consequently, you already possess, by means of your incomprehensibly free gift of holistic spirituality an interconnection with the ultimate therapist, the divine physician of body and soul. When this interconnectivity is appropriated through a conjoined effort of your praxis (reflective action), an inner dialogue with yourself, and God's omniscient inspiration, self-motivation will become a quotidian experience.

Although it is true that without God we can do nothing, there is a certain expectation in the divorce healing process, which insists upon the victim's active participation in correlation with God's Will. In one sense that is the purpose of this brief but crucial chapter.

God is always willing to help direct and encourage your healing, however, it is incumbent upon you to minimally provide self-motivation. Activity not passivity is obligatory for genuine divorce healing. Seeking God's assistance in "getting yourself off the proverbial couch" through physical activities, intellectual stimulation and soulful (faith based prayer) will lead to self-motivation.

As referenced in the previous paragraph, an inner dialogue, a type of contemplative self-interrogation, is a highly effective tool in the self-motivational enterprise. Perhaps, you have already embarked upon the multiple queries of this self-reflective approach. If you have not, the kairotic moment, for inner dialogue has now commenced. This self-motivating intellectual activity is a simple as it is innate. Your virtually interminable thought generating mind incessantly engenders ideas in a singular yet rapidly dynamic motion. The inner dialogue becomes a deeply private personal self-conversation which probes your responses to inherently provocative divorce related questions. This dialogue becomes a barometer allowing you to ascertain the level of your motivation to determinedly heal from an unanticipated divorce.

Analytical questions which focus with laser-like precision on determinative issues at the crux of your divorce healing progress or the lack thereof are extremely revelatory. For example, by simply asking yourself, "Do I really desire to heal from the tragedy of my unexpected divorce?" This direct question will access a plethora of hidden concerns. This focused question, the answer to which appears absurdly obvious, may divulge a profusion of undetected intricacies and nuances. It may manifest a genuine lack of motivation to heal. It may, in some bizarre manner, signal desperation to return to the former spouse. It may demonstrate a maturational deficiency capitulating to the inner child. In essence, the inner dialogue, promotes the benefit of self-confrontation thereby allowing self-motivation to evolve from potency to activity. The conclusion represents itself: the inner dialogue is a reasonable and responsible method to advance the requisite self-motivation mandated in your divorce healing progress.

Your unanticipated divorce is a peculiar matter. By their very nature peculiar matters require peculiar responses. The reader is asked to hold a receptively open mind when approaching the unique forthcoming proposition. This volume presents the eminent equation of the distinguished theoretical physicist, Albert Einstein, $E=mc^2$, as another instrument to sustain self-motivation. Recall that, for the victim of divorce, utilizing self-motivational techniques will encourage one to abscond from the vitiating paralysis of a lethargic lifestyle. This holistic activity is mandatory for divorce healing progress. Allow the following metaphoric representation to serve as an allegorical illustration focused on divorce healing self-motivation using the discovered physics of Dr. Einstein's renowned equation.

Consider yourself to be a universe whose constituents are your body, mind, and soul. Extrapolating from Dr. Einstein's equation—Energy equals mass times the velocity of light squared—to your "personal universe," perhaps the following analogy will be determinative. The Energy in the exemplified equation is your ability to actually do work (to literally or metaphorically "get off the couch"). This energy is equivalent to your Mass, which is a measure of resistance to acceleration when a force is applied to it. This Mass may be interpreted as the weight of the intensity of your personal divorce related concerns, which impose themselves upon you and pull back. The Mass is then multiplied by the velocity of light squared. The speed of light, the most rapid universal constant, is being expressed to its second power. This "squared speed of light" may depict your illuminative desire to act to a second power of itself (a typology of the light of Christ) in resistance to remaining dormant, immobile or stationary. The conclusive point is that both your Mass and Energy are the same physical entity and can be changed into each other. Ironically, the Energy referenced above is determined to be kinetic energy, a form of energy that an object has by reason of its motion.

Indubitably, the above paragraph is obviously designed as a highly stretched analogy. However, it all begins with (E) energy (kinetic energy.) The source of this energy, in this illustrative metaphoric example, is realistically derived from your "second wind." The Hebrew word for this second wind or breath or spirit is *ruach*.

This *ruach* can be interpreted as the Holy Spirit, the divine director of your holistic spirituality. The Holy Spirit can and will breathe into you the kinetic energy for your requisite self-motivation by means of prayerful petition. The One who wrote the precise mathematics and physics of the universe (from the smallest sub-atomic particles to the immensity of an inflationary cosmos) into being, having fine-tuned its sustainability and continual expansion is "groaning" in creative response to your desired self-motivational needs. The Holy Spirit is not dissimilar to a loving and very tolerant parent, who may occasionally disapprove of her or his child's behavior, yet absolutely loves that child. This Holy Spirit knows that your lethargy is symptomatic of a deeper issue. Only the energy provided by the Holy Spirit (as the ruach) in tandem with the efforts of your holistic spirituality can energize any personal resistance to continued motivation toward divorce healing progress.

Recall that the focus of this chapter is to mitigate and/or ideally alleviate the detrimental effects on appropriate divorce healing resulting from one's inclination toward the temptations of a lethargic, non-motivated lifestyle. The intent has been, and will continue to be, the provision of non-perfunctory, non-radical and non-vapid *suggested* considerations encouraging the reader's self-motivation. Hence, the following ten reflective analyses will be pertinent codicils to the informative material thus far presented. The hope is to encourage an ardent passion in "moving" forward respecting the necessity for a motivation replete with unanticipated divorce healing recommendations.

ONE

For those individuals determined to heal from an unanticipated divorce, self-motivation is compulsory. Therefore, consider the reality that *idleness breeds discontent*. Proper divorce healing is predicated upon the frequency of focused healthy activity. The temptations to diminish your motivational efforts will be profuse. However, you have an eternity to rest, now is the time for strategic efficacious exertion. Your positive attitude aligned with authentic activities will yield, indeed will increase, the likelihood of incremental success in divorce healing viability.

Tranquility of body, mind, and soul will come as a gift of the Holy Spirit as you are created anew. However, the reverse is also the case. If you choose to sit idly accomplishing nothing in the divorce healing realm that is exactly what you will achieve. Realistically, doing nothing can produce only nothing. Arguably, one may readily make the case that, discontent is the only by-product of the idle life style. The human body, mind, and soul were super-intelligently designed for vigorous activity. The very passions that you possess are interwoven with your actions. Philosophically, it has been debated as to which is the initial response, human passion or human action. For the divorce victim, the less healthy the activity, the more atrophied the determination. Idleness not only breeds discontent it also degenerates the mind and gradually incapacitates the will. The consequence is a virtually imperceptible acquiescence to the demonic force of complete resignation.

In order to surmount the malignant effects caused by the debilitating triumvirate of idleness, discontent, and waning self-motivation an intently tenacious strategy is warranted. You absolutely must force yourself to physically, mentally, or soulfully alter your state of being. Elevate yourself by freely choosing to adjust the direction of your inactive mode. Just do it.

Get off that material or metaphorical couch and compel yourself to either do or think or pray something healthy and healing. Ask for the Wisdom of God, Jesus Christ, by means of His Holy Spirit to provide just one self-motivational idea. Then expeditiously act upon it. For example, ask where you might go, or what you might read, or whom you might text, merely allow the triune God to quickly remedy the nemesis with one potent activity. The more frequently that you use this strategy the better prepared you will be for future bouts with the ill-conceived triumvirate. God will always answer your sincere request, not necessarily through a theophany but by inducing a candid and direct thought (an insight) within your mind. Your only obligation is to demonstrate gratitude by immediately acting on it. This intelligible yet tenacious strategy while relatively simplistic in format requires faith filled belief and frequent practice. Using your holistic spirituality will decimate the doldrums and refocus your divorce healing progress.

TWO

By the lacerations, the cross and the resurrection of Jesus Christ you are healed. Recall from the previous chapter that the triune God subsists in an "eternal (timeless) present." For the Father, Son and Holy Spirit, who are the one economic and immanent Trinitarian God, there exists neither past nor future time. While all creation lives its life in successive moments, the immanent Trinity exists only in a perpetual "now." Of course, there is only *one* Trinity, hence the immanent Trinity is the economic Trinity and vice versa. This reality is beyond our finite comprehension yet it is a doctrinal tenet of the Christian monotheistic faith. Only the God/Man, Jesus Christ, freely took on a human nature while maintaining His divine nature. The point being elucidated here, for the member of the unanticipated divorced community, is that Jesus Christ is fully God and fully human.

He was/is totally involved with all the implications of being a human person including suffering and empathy. The only exception for Christ is that He is completely sinless. This union of Christ's divine nature with His human nature is referred to by Christians as the hypostatic union. Christ freely accepted the infinitely loving holy Will of His heavenly Father to offer Himself as a sacrifice for all human sin. His personal human sacrifice infinitely overshadowed the Hebrew traditional animal sacrifices of repentance for sin. Hence, Jesus Christ physically walked the territories of Israel approximately two thousand years ago. Christ was fully God and fully human. He was a human person like us in every way except for sin. He was incarnate of the Virgin Mary overshadowed by the Holy Spirit and raised to work with His foster father, Joseph, as a carpenter growing to adulthood in age, wisdom and God's favor. Christ's mission was the ransom and redemption of all humanity from sin through His incomprehensible suffering. This occurred in human time approximately two thousand years ago. His passion, death on the cross, and resurrection from the dead, once for all has been "finished." At this moment, and unto eternity, He is fully alive in a glorified human body yet simultaneously is consubstantially equal in every way with God the Father and God the Holy Spirit in His divine personhood.

For the victim of an unanticipated divorce, the above doctrinal information is a concisely incipient theology relevant to your divorce healing. What is being shared is that in Christ's passion (the immensity of Christ's freely chosen physical and emotional suffering) He has *already* healed you from all the pain and suffering of your divorce! By all His afflictions, humiliations, lacerations, tormented crucifixion and excruciating death on the cross, Christ has taken on all human sin and suffering. Christ has already healed you from the horrific pain of your unanticipated divorce by assuming all personal suffering. Today, whether you agree or not Christ has already healed your sin and pain. This incomprehensible sacrificial oblation has healed you (two thousand years ago) from the anguish of your unexpected divorce. If the God/Man has freely chosen to do this for you, how can you possibly not motivate yourself to become motivated? Of course, you must accept and believe this sacred reality and then act in accordance with it.

The resurrection of Christ from death is the "proof" that He has conquered all sin and that by his lacerations you are healed. We victims of divorce must walk by faith and not necessarily by sight. Rely on the God-given gift of your holistic spirituality to reflectively meditate on all of the above and then motivate yourself toward healthy healing activities. Gratitude for Christ's unselfish, highly motivated, self-sacrifice, whereby, the God/Man "divorces" Himself from the alternative to do nothing for your healing should profoundly move even the most lethargic heart. If, you genuinely accept this second reflective consideration toward self-motivation, know that you *are* already healed by Christ's bruises, suffering, death and resurrection. Then, it is the kairotic moment for you to "get off the couch" and ask for the triune God's motivational help.

This simple petition, because of Christ's sacrifice, will reenergize your divorce healing progress. If this healing is a conundrum because you continue to anguish over the effects of unexpected divorce this is because you have not accepted Christ's healing in its complexity. What is needed is an impassioned faith suffused with an intractable determination to do whatever is required for your divorce healing. Conjoin your current sufferings with those of Christ.

THREE

The self-motivational question: "Do I want my former spouse to continue control over me as I numbly vegetate on the couch?" For the victim of an unanticipated divorce, who is determinedly serious about a healthy healing experience, the presented question must be directly addressed. Apologies are rendered to the reader since some terse yet poignant remarks are necessitated in approaching said correct response. This particular reflective analysis concentrates on the non-sexual but definitively unconscious masochistic tendencies possessed by certain disoriented victims of an unexpected divorce. Many of these victims exigently long for self-motivational activities to move forward in the divorce healing enterprise but simultaneously employ a bizarre self-induced desire to relinquish their personal freedom.

Unfortunately, yet realistically, these addled victims abdicate control of their "divorced lives" in unadulterated vegetation emanating only meandering thoughts of the former spouse. Conversely, the former spouse is normally unaware of the mastery, which they somehow possess over their now divorced former spouse. While the divorce victim withers away numbly deteriorating on the "couch" of her or his life, they also masochistically tolerate the pleasure of the pain caused by the former spouse. As puppets to an incognizant puppet master, they surrender control of their human authenticity to the divorce's initiator. Indeed, the mind of the divorced victim is often an odd sanctuary. And the mind of the "divorcer" is very often abnormally preoccupied with her or his own selfish and narcissistic motives to be cognizant of this despicable situation.

As a divorce victim, you must absolutely never allow any human being to control your personal consciousness. Your awareness of your awareness is a personal and sacred issue. Your ability to know that you know that you know is a profoundly private matter. The freedom of thought to choose the "thinkables" attained by your personally authentic actions, attitudes, emotions, and perceptions is pristine. They belong solely to you and ground your personhood. You own those personal boundaries, which, to some extent, define your uniquely individual personality. It is abhorrent for you to concede the time necessary to self-motivate and possibly begin divorce healing by remaining transfixed to memories of your former spouse.

A cardinal sin of the healthy divorce healing enterprise is to allow your former spouse, as a result of uselessly idle reminiscences, to violate the sanctity of your consciousness. Do you actually allow yourself to draw some twisted pleasure from this inane suffering and lack of self-control? The more august insult is derived from the fact that your former spouse is unaware and unaffected by this self-induced and absurdly permitted illogical mind control. Simply stated, your lack of appropriate self-motivational activity permits the former spouse to unknowingly become the provocateur of this emotional carnage while you idly vegetate. If this is the reader's current quandary, the following basic tenets, when faithfully applied, will help embolden you to work on remedying the dysfunctional nature of this flawed tendency.

Initially, as with all divorce healing concerns or issues, you must begin with a brief prayer of guidance to the Holy Spirit. Prudently utilize your God-given holistic spirituality (body, mind, and soul) in an assertive, directed and positively determined manner. Your stringent determination to correctly answer the above propaedeutic self-motivational question is mandatory. The only correct response is "absolutely not!" Therefore, focus with laser-like precision upon the entire gamut of your holistic spirituality as preparation for daily confrontation with this contentious issue.

Secondly, do not be abnormally frenzied by the consequent admonitions and consternations of the above paragraphs. However, it is of paramount importance to your mental health in the divorce healing process to correctly address this highly significant concern. Therefore, redefine yourself as being the one who will not succumb to any inclination to forego control of your "new" albeit divorced life. Your mantra must be, "I control myself by my thoughts, words, and actions."

Thirdly, if you want to alter this debilitating attitude, change all controlling negative behaviors. This is truly a herculean task but consider the old saw, "you eat an elephant one bite at a time." Move forward gradually yet prudently progress a tad every day. Recall, if you surrender control in faith and effort through your holistic spirituality to the triune God success is assured. If you surrender control to your egocentric and incognizant former spouse only the lair of a depressed attitude awaits. Compel yourself to no longer merely endure as a languid entity, flex and strain your psychological and holistically spiritual muscularity and "get off the couch."

Finally, work on becoming compatible with your inner self. You have experienced a considerable amount of trepidation, now is the appropriate time to take action and live in harmony with yourself. Harmony, in this sense, is an interior peace that results from the confidence of motivating yourself to actively "work through" the difficulties of an unanticipated divorce. As you positively self-motivate, your confidence, and therefore, that necessary inner harmony, will help continually facilitate the divorce healing progress. When you commit to becoming the architect of your life, healthy healing activity begins manifesting itself. Respectfully, your only genuine responsibility is to yourself and the triune God.

FOUR

The daily use of body, mind, and soul in small but positive healing activities will produce significant cumulative effects on your healthy divorce healing. For the victim of an unanticipated divorce, who struggles to find healthy self-motivational activities, this reflective analysis can be prolific. It would be a fruitless consideration to suggest that your "universe" is not encompassed by a plethora of quotidian divorce healing opportunities. The favorable circumstances that occur during the course of the average divorce victim's day are virtually limitless. If one simply keeps her or his spiritual "antennae" sensitive it is in essence well-nigh impossible not to encounter divorce healing motivations.

Your world is pregnant with circumstances, people, and situations which are ripe with opportune moments to develop self-motivational skills. These skills will be formative in furthering your divorce healing progress. Simple small activities, brief personal encounters, seemingly meaningless events if acted upon in a positive manner are healing ventures. The magnitude of the act is insignificant. The significance of the act is drawn from your intentionality. Divorce healing is incremental. Therefore, each small positive personal activity ameliorates the divorced victim. If you are resolute in the determined attitude to "get off the couch" know that this is done *gradually and with holistic effort* by most fatigued divorce victims. Internalize this apropos African proverb, "If you think that the small events in your life are insignificant, try to sleep with a mosquito in the tent."

What motivates an infant to crawl or a toddler to walk? What innate desire stimulates a baby to communicate? What antecedent motive is the incentive for these maturational inclinations in the mind of a child? What is it that prompts non-verbal to attempted verbal communication within the human offspring? For decades, cognitive development specialists in the complex domain of child maturation have debated the above concerns. Your particular reflective analysis treats these questions in terms of self-motivational techniques designated for the adult periodically flummoxed by lethargic trepidations. Simply stated, if an infant can self-motivate, then so also can you. The prevalent components of the desire to motivate yourself toward healthy divorce healing alternatives versus merely "lying on the couch" will now be briefly considered.

The infant, toddler, or child that develops the intricate cognitive and neuromuscular dexterity to talk or walk must overcome multiple failures prior to achieving a modicum of success. Through determined trial and error, achieving a goal farther and faster, curiosity, daily practice, discovery, exploration, imitation, natural playful activities, observation, real needs, and self-induced wants—the accumulation and repetition of all of these procedures ultimately but gradually impel success. Consider the human child's motivational determination as your template. This assignment is uncomplicated since you competently experienced these occurrences in your own childhood.

Today, as the victim of an unanticipated divorce, who confronts flaccid motivational enthusiasm, learn from your own childhood history. You are replete with the identical motivations as a corollary to your childhood. Now, however, you are substantially more mentally agile, experienced and prudent. Therefore, if you could self-motivate then, self-motivation for today must simply follow the same basic determined pattern. Do not be embarrassed nor intimidated by easing into those critical "baby steps" which will collectively accumulate into divorce healing self-motivational episodes. However, it is obligatory, at this inchoate stratum of your unexpected and undeserved divorce healing to utilize the holistically spiritual exercises (of body, mind, and soul) to enhance impending progress.

FIVE

To self-motivate compel yourself to act with enthusiasm. Simply stated, this particular reflective analysis contends that to be enthusiastic you must "act" with enthusiasm. You currently possess considerable experience in this venue. Many times throughout your life you have forced enthusiasm to demonstrate itself. For example, during or prepping for a significant interview, or when preparing to sell a product or service, or even the daily task of lumbering into your job, each of these experiences (and many more) have required your penchant to manifest an enthusiastic attitude.

The fact is when one acts with enthusiasm, one can become enthusiastic. Innately you possess the potential which is necessary to be activated. There is no self-deception or specious emotion warranted in the above declarations. You will not unpack, in this commentary, any direct relationship to personal mind games. Rather this analysis truthfully provides insight into attitudinal adjustments necessary for the fatigued and lackadaisical victim of an unexpected divorce.

If this is your current state, once you perceive the positive comments of others regarding a newly demonstrated enthusiastic lifestyle, lethargy will be summarily replaced with supplementary self-motivating enthusiasm. Therefore, you have absolutely nothing to lose. Simply enthusiastically immerse your entire holistic being (body, mind, and soul) into the appropriate divorce healing enterprise and you will become incrementally more enthusiastic and self-motivated. Confer with the Holy Spirit to effuse you with a cascade of ebullient holistic exercises. Recall, for example, that reasonably vigorous walking, laughing, feelings of pride, even consuming a bit of dark chocolate, releases dopamine, endorphins, and serotonin each a God-given cost free natural energy/enthusiasm booster.

If you are skeptical of this approach, seek out the etymology of the term enthusiasm. It is in flawless correlation with your holistic spirituality and the triune God. The term is derived from the Greek "*enthousiasmos*," Anglicized to mean "having God within" or being "God inspired" or living "God possessed." Is this not the core of your holistic spirituality inspired by and in relationship with God the Holy Spirit? There can be nothing fallacious in the meaning and utility of this term for the dedicated victim of divorce healing. The concern, for some divorce victims, is the proper understanding of the term as employed in this chapter. Hence, for the purposes expressed herein, enthusiasm is not the spurious falsehood of doing double flips with feigned excitement. It is not the pretense of fabricated emotion or action. It is the genuine reality that is *suggesting* to the indolent divorce victim the old saw "a journey of one thousand miles begins with a first step." Isn't it time for you to take that first step by bolstering your enthusiasm and resisting the lure of idleness posed by that material or metaphorical couch? Within an aggregation of productive time, you will come to the realization that initiating your enthusiasm, which is quite likely a by-product of "the endorphin effect" has been inculcated within your God-given human nature to energize enjoyment in fully living the gift of life.

SIX

Pray for energy. In the dedicated divorce healing process, occasions frequently transpire that stymie one's ardor to continually elicit evermore physical and psychic stamina. It is not uncommon to temporarily lose the vitality that has prevailed against multiple obstacles. The reader must not succumb to the inclination that no other divorce victim has ever had to endure these identical temporary impediments. Remind yourself frequently that divorce healing progress is a quotidian effort. Simultaneously, prompt yourself to acknowledge that while you may appear tired and lonely the indefatigable Holy Spirit is always present. Hence, briefly but potently pray for the necessary energy to overcome any temporary hindrance. Recall, that Christ, Himself, encourages each of us to ask, and be prepared to receive, to seek out and consequently find, persistently knock and His door will be made to open.

Jesus Christ, the Wisdom of God, presciently understands the entirety of your exhaustion. Christ's road to Mt. Calvary was the most exhausting event ever endured. His incomparable fatigue dwarfs the totality of any human suffering. This was caused by Christ's free choice to endure incomprehensible physical and emotional pain while accepting the sins of *all* humanity. Yet embarrassed, physically broken, scourged, and thrice fallen, His Holy Spirit energized a plodding continuance toward an excruciating crucifixion. Most theologians suggest that His death came after continually suffering hours of asphyxiation. With these macabre thoughts in mind, the astute reader will observe both the devotion and inexorable energy which Jesus prayed to possess. Respectfully, when lethargy overcomes your fervor to gradually energize the holistic spirituality that you possess, connect your lack of vigor with the strength and determination of Christ. Simply stated, adhere to the stated reflective analysis: pray for energy.

"Jesus, give me strength!"

"Jesus, give me energy, now!"

"Holy Spirit, direct my thoughts!" These concise yet efficacious prayers are not the least bit onerous. However, they possess the spiritual volume of a gold bar, small in mass yet containing abundant matter and weight.

Prayer, of course, is communication with the triune God. It is a matter of candidly and devotedly speaking directly to God then listening for God's response in momentary quietude. Therefore, if you need the energy to "get off the couch" and physically or mentally or soulfully activate your holistic spirituality, then pray for it. Pray briefly and sincerely that you are given the insight to become energetic enough to be guided toward healthy, healing, non-toxic activity. Energy is the capacity to do work with vigor. Focus on simplicity of prayer and aggressive listening for God's response. No prayer is too inane or elementary neither is any prayer excessively complex for God's unrestricted omniscience.

One of the issues confronting the victim of an unanticipated divorce is omitting prayer in times of need. Universally, there appear more errors of omission than of co-mission. You are graced with the superabundant gift of a holistic spirituality. Frequently this gift of a relationship with the Trinity is overlooked and unused at critical moments in your life. So rather than seek God's omnipotence and omniscience, many victims errantly choose to either do nothing or try resolving a problem with their own finite strategies. This grievous omission generally results in confusion which deepens frustration and consequently vitiates self-motivational action. However, to pray for the energy to actually move toward a healing activity or a self-conceptually healthy behavior will be answered often in that moment (insight). It will come as a mental clarification, a perspicuity, which deeply resonates with the prayerful divorce victim. Be advised that God will often answer each of us through ideas emanating from other people, life's circumstances, and the "stuff" of our daily events. As a loving and prudent parent directing the best option for her or his child, God will always answer either with a yes, a no, or a not at this moment. Yet nothing will be answered by God, if nothing is sought from God even by the most sincere divorce victim. Miracles can occur; however, they are frequently the result of fervent prayer and the incomprehensible Will of God.

The converse of the above is also the case. Occasionally, many divorce victims have a tendency to consider our unconditionally loving Trinity as an automaton (a type of mechanized godbot), a preprogrammed robot made in humanity's image. This "coin slot" God is conjured up to be a divine candy machine. In this errant scenario, the victim simply inserts her or his coin of petition into the slot of God's infinite love machine and then selects and receives the candied choice.

While this scenario is obviously ludicrous and hyperbolic, often we omit the relational component of our holistic spirituality. We selfishly consider only our wants and not the real personal needs presciently observed by God. Recall, God's eternally present mode of existence allows for your precise needs (e.g., healthy, self-motivating activities) to have already been addressed. God's foreknowledge apprehends the entire scope of your existence. The triune God mysteriously knows the full reality of the authentic "you" prior to your conception. Simultaneously, you must never omit the authenticity of our God who neither frivolously nor randomly dispenses your callow wants or self-indulgent appetites. Therefore, have faith in the absolute reality that God has provided the apropos energy in answer to your prayer. Your most respectful responsibility is to thank God by actually "getting off the couch" and continuing the divorce healing process.

SEVEN

"Get off the couch" for yourself, your children, family, friends and as an example to other divorced colleagues. You self-motivate by demonstrating to others, through healthy actions and comments, your definitive progress in the divorce healing enterprise. This comes as a highly respected reflective analysis because it reinforces your positive development and allows others to feel more comfortable being collaterally damaged by the ramifications of the divorce. The abhorrent ripple effect of your unanticipated divorce selfishly calculated and then insisted upon must be endured. Since, personal historical experiences can occur only unidirectionally, you cannot reverse the past. However, you can alter the negative effects of an unforeseen divorce by living a *new* life exclusive

of your former spouse. This life altering determined attitude will alleviate much of the detrimental impact forcibly imposed on those closest to you by the heinous action of your former spouse. "Get off the couch" to shelter them, to console them, to ameliorate their confusion and frustration. Your loved ones have been perplexed far too long. They each know, in the depths of their hearts, that you are not the person responsible for this adversity. Yet your positive actions and healthy motivations will provide incalculable restoration to their disoriented feelings. Their observations of you and your obvious healing progress should be the apex of any obligatory self-motivational inspiration. Consequently, the most prudent methods to control the catastrophic ripple effect of your unsolicited divorce, is the result of an activated holistic spirituality conjoined with the affirmative observations of loved ones. Only you, by the God-given grace of your operative holistic spirituality, can make this happen.

Your divorce healing efforts will transcend the egregious machinations schemed by your former spouse. The potency of your God-given holistic spirituality when activated does not allow for mere ambling through life or philosophical ponderings about it. You have a premier ebullient Spirit-filled opportunity to become a role model to other divorced victims.

While there is considerable veracity exposited in the comprehensive taxonomy of learning, level one is the procurement of knowledge. Human cognitive development is contingent upon multiple conditions. For purposes of this reflective analysis, one of the most potent and enduring is the acquisition of knowledge through observation. In the laborious quotidian endeavor to penetrate the divorce healing challenge, you are being meticulously scrutinized by colleagues and friends of a similar ilk. You are not only defined by your actions they inherently become an example for others. The reader can be assured that you are either a divorce healing source of encouragement or a disappointment to those in your coterie. This situation, while not specifically chosen, is your reality. However, few circumstances can be more self-motivating and rewarding. You grow and others, known and unknown, begin to take root. Further amplification of this modeling type behavior will accrue as you become more profoundly cognizant of your resultant positive effects on others. Simply "getting off the couch" has an inestimable affect upon your divorce healing and potentially that of untold others.

A brief consideration is treated at this juncture for those unanticipated divorce victims who are blessed with children. Your child's age is not a factor. There is only one absolutely critical question to be addressed. Do you fully comprehend the immense beneficial effects of your self-motivational actions on the child or children that God has so very graciously consecrated to your care? They are happy and well-balanced when you are observed by them to be the same. They love both parents and perceive the divorce situation as unusual but can gradually adjust themselves to it *if* no acrimony is observed. This is *your* parental obligation and you cannot control the ill-conceived actions or attitude of a former spouse. Consequently, if you only "got off the couch" for the benefit and well-being of your children, that is more than ample reason. You can do things together, spend quality time together, buy "things" for them, all of this matters little if they sense your inner angst, ennui, and lethargy. Recall, age is not the factor, your personal unrest or state of agitation can be observed by a toddler or adult child. You are capable of communication by multiple techniques. The best communication is often non-verbal. Quality learning is rarely auditory. It is most effective in the visual realm. Hence, the mere observation of your authentic happiness and self-motivated activity is enough to comfort and satisfy the most precocious child.

Do not allow the "unanticipated divorce syndrome" to affect your children. You exponentially increase their opportunity to acclimate through the morass of this tragic event by demonstrating your positive evolution. Your self-motivational activities elucidated by personal demonstrable growth, augurs well for them. Can anything be more self-motivating for the truly loving unexpectedly divorced parent?

Whether or not the reader has children, the observation of your comfort in this newly formulated lifestyle is contagious. It bodes well for your children, family, friends, and those confronting a similar life altering situation. Fear and pity are substantially mitigated and may be thoroughly alleviated by means of continuous conscious and subconscious positive observations. However, it is only through healthy self-motivating activities that you can visually demonstrate the comfortable freedom found in your newly created life. All of the above presupposes the sincere use of your holistic spirituality in a candidly profound interrelationship with the motivational ideas inspired within you by the triune God. You need only a modicum of faith and straightforward communication with the Holy Spirit to become self-motivated enough to "get off the couch."

EIGHT

In your weakness, you find the most strength. The astonishing paradox which initiates this reflective analysis has been paraphrased from the thought of St. Paul. Paul, a pinnacle of purpose driven self-motivation, experienced immense emotional and physical pain, in a determined effort to spread fledgling Christianity to the known Gentile world. His keen understanding and application of holistic spirituality is virtually unparalleled in the annals of Christendom. Paul, in his prudence and love for Christ, used his body, mind, and soul to continually motivate himself through severe trials. Even while withstanding horrific pain, he compelled himself to write thirteen New Testament letters to motivate fledgling Christianity. The victim of an unanticipated divorce, who is rigorously focused on healing, yet periodically lapses into flaccidity or lethargy, will glean much wisdom by drilling down into the opening paradoxical reflective analysis paraphrased from St. Paul.

Simply stated, the triune God is exponentially present to strengthen you particularly in your weakest moments. The effects of Original sin are diabolically alluring to our human propensity toward self-indulgence as an attractive albeit errant alternative in the consistency necessitated by divorce healing progress. Given this human condition and its repercussions, your dependence upon the almighty, omnipotent, unrestricted Trinitarian God provides incomprehensible divine strength when you are most feeble. Temporarily, immersed at the lowest ebb of self-motivation is when you have the most power to deal with divorce healing complexities. Christ, who is omnipresent, has an inexplicable predilection for those stricken by intense weakness. In God's omniscience, the horizon of your frailty is observed and in God's omnipotence you are graced with super abundant strength to overcome both weak-heartedness and weak-mindedness. This comes to reality as the result of God's infinite love conjoined with your holistic spirituality.

Recapitulated, the triune God is most available to provide you with copious amounts of strength during your weakest periods. This actuality is realized through your faith in God's interrelationship with you in the depths of that holistic spirituality. All victims of an unforeseen divorce must fully consent to progress by faith and not by logic or serendipity. A brief anecdotal scenario may provide a modest analogy at this juncture, especially for the skeptic.

If you are boarding a flight to Punta Cana, you inherently trust the airplane's mechanics, structure, pilot and the fact that you will safely arrive at your specific destination. You will probably never meet these people again and quite likely never fly on that same airplane. However, you innately trust all of the above to definitively meet your expectations. Now, if this is true of finite humanity and materials and destinations—why is it not infinitely more trustworthy/faith filled to place an equal or greater belief in God's promises? If the pilot says that you are flying at thirty thousand feet or that the weather in Punta Cana is eighty-seven degrees or that the flight will arrive twenty-three minutes ahead of schedule do you believe this unknown person? Why then, as the victim of an unanticipated divorce, would you have the most remote difficulty believing that in your weakness you find the most strength within the infinitely loving omnipotence of God? The reader must faithfully recognize that you have already been baptized with The Spirit of courage, strength and self-motivation. Hence, when you are weak, strength will abound. This is not due to happenstance or random contingency. It is another gift from God.

In sum, when you fall into the abyss of emphatically low spirits regarding your divorce healing progress, The Holy Spirit is most thoroughly present to assist with an abundant infusion of potent alternatives and *suggestions*. Your feeble attitude will be reconfigured to assume a plethora of pragmatic holistic motivational concepts. This is a tacit indication of "the unconditional Lover" cascading incredible amounts of unexpected strength into your entire being at its lowest ebb. In harrowing moments "the supernatural specific gravity" of God's aurous substantial opulence compacts your feet of clay which now become firmly implanted in the density of copious Trinitarian grace. Consequently, the exercises of your holistic spirituality should welcome the adversity of divorce healing.

In your weakest moments, you are wonderfully compelled to rely for undaunted guidance upon the laser focused omnipotence of God. Therefore, when you are in severe pain the opportunity for the greatest motivational gain is absolutely available in, with, and through Christ.

NINE

Commitment to persistence and perseverance is essential for your divorce healing progress. The implication of this reflective analysis mandates that the determined single-minded divorce victim is required to "get off the couch." The correlation between healthy self-motivated activities of body, mind, and soul and devoted divorce healing are unmistakably apparent. Therefore, if you are absolutely adamant in your divorce healing determination, persistence is a tacit passion.

If, like the author, you possess a propensity to "skip" an occasional workout at the gym or sporadically indulge in tasty but unhealthy snacks, we can momentarily rationalize our imprudent behavior. However, this is not a methodology to be endorsed within the determined divorce healing process. We, veterans of the ongoing divorce healing struggle, realize that "the evil one" can craft a salacious situation or event to gradually mitigate your commitment. In your finitude and imperfection you may occasionally succumb to his temptations. However, the impact will be vastly more damaging to your healing progress than merely missing a workout or fudging on your diet.

A day lost in lethargy can be lethal and may quickly metastasize like a cancer of toxic inactivity. Therefore, ask for the power of the Calvary bound thrice-fallen Christ, to re-commit and learn resiliency from this lapse of focus. Be assured that "off days or events" will become radically reduced as you observe the payoff of persistence through the explosive energy of the Holy Spirit providing you with a "second wind." Simply stated, whenever you fall get back up and start again, recall the resolute determination of the persevering infant.

You must realize that appropriate divorce healing allows no time for rationalizing errant behaviors as being innocuous. If you are going to heal from an unanticipated divorce, then daily perseverance is compulsory. The etymology of the term persevere is derived from the Latin meaning "strictly abiding to an action even if it is severe." The reader must also recognize that the terms persistence and perseverance, while often considered interchangeable, are not in actuality identical expressions yet both are essential. Hence, while the terms are not counterpoised, they are rudimentary toward the generation of divorce healing commitment. One is "persistent" by demonstrating continuity of *endurance* in spite of frequent *difficulties*. However, one is "perseverant" by maintaining a *steadfast* attitude despite *incessant delays* in achieving a goal. Clearly, both are tacit prerequisites of a bona fide personal commitment to your divorce healing endeavors.

The triune God is conclusively involved in your commitment to both persistence and perseverance. Furthermore, God is always present as a type of intrinsic and/or extrinsic "force" either in a shadowed nuance or a palpably lucid manner available to strengthen your commitment. In an obvious anthropomorphism, God "despises" your vulnerabilities and desperately desires "to pull you off the couch." An adjunct to your commitment is a prayerful seeking of God's infinite Wisdom (which is Jesus Christ) whenever endurance or steadfastness begins to wane. Your absolutely genuine assistance regarding all issues proposed in this book comes by first seeking God's perfect direction and motivation.

As you intuit personal continued success, persistence and perseverance will correlate in complementarity with the three components (body, mind, and soul) of your holistic spirituality. Eventually, you will enthusiastically perceive this healthy self-motivating accomplishment. However, this is a quotidian task which becomes easier and more natural through praxis. Only then are you realistically reinforcing your commitment to both persistence and perseverance in the divorce healing enterprise.

Recall, that persistence is explicit in its focus upon your endurance during difficulties. Perseverance is explicit in its expectation of your steadfastness when frequent delays in divorce healing progress will transpire. The prudent reader will adamantly remain focused on her or his commitment through persistence, perseverance, and the inspirational motivation of the Holy Spirit. When lethargy approaches immediately ask for the omnipotent energy of your unconditionally loving God. Having received that super-abundant impetus of divinized motivation obligates you in a respectful gratitude "to get off the couch."

TEN

The final reflective analysis is yet another pragmatic recommendation, a fundamental self-motivational consideration and technique to help you "get off the couch." The reader clearly understands that it would be the quintessence of hyperbole to imply the ergonomics of human engineering and muscle memory by entitling this chapter "How to Get Off the Couch" and then offering a methodology! Respectfully, all of this chapter's ten reflective analyses are seriously proffered to the determined victim of an unanticipated divorce in an effort to provide proven considerations which can activate your holistically spiritual potential. Ideally the strategy is to stimulate self-motivational activities that will enhance your divorce healing process.

Moving forward, the allocated designation of this tenth reflective analysis is ironically both simple and complex. *Just for today!* No human person can alter even one scintilla of her or his previous history. We all endure within a timeline of events that is continuing forward. Even contemporary physics cannot compel time to regress. Indubitably contingent upon a plethora of events and manners you are the composition aggregated by your past experiences. However, you were not created with the capacity to literally change your historical past.

Contemporaneously, no human person possesses foreknowledge. Occasionally, a hypothetically educated guess may come to pass, but this is normally induced from the purview of science rather than the augury of your personal future. We are not designed by God to predict, let alone conclusively "know" *our* individual human destiny, futurity or subsequent temporality. For example, stating the obvious fact that someday I will die does not equate to foreknowledge rather it is the eventual condition of all currently corporeal enduring entities. We all possess the theological virtue of hope optimistically aspiring to experience eternity with the Trinity. Yet despite the efficacy of hope it is still not a predictive measure of future manifestations.

Each of us must live in the successive moments of the present which aggregates as a result of our quotidian experiences. Hence, as the conscientious reader may have already discerned, daily success within the divorce healing enterprise is contingent upon many requirements. However, each of these activities and requirements must be managed from day to day. Therefore, the reflective analysis, *just for today*, is most appropriate.

Recall, that the one God subsists in three distinct manners of subsisting within an eternal present. You and I have a historically unalterable past, no real knowledge of the future and can only live in the temporality of each successive corporeal present moment. The point, particularly for the divorce victim, is to live well prepared, event by event, throughout the course of each day. In this sense, you must approach your divorce as a daily gift, offering the realistic opportunity for a new life!

The healthy and unhealthy experiences that you confront or confront you each day serve to strengthen your divorce healing progress. With divine Wisdom and your holistic spirituality being activated, you will evolve and learn from both the positive and negative events of each day. Practical real-world life experience seems to imply that we extrapolate more knowledge deeper and quicker from negative encounters than from the positives. This debatable reality does not mean to suggest that you focus on negative propositions in your divorce healing. It does stringently intimate that the natural issues which affect the victim of divorce are best handled incrementally within the *just for today* mode.

If you are physically and/or emotionally exhausted by the remnant of your divorce and the requisite essentials of the healing process, supplemental energy will not be discovered in more sleep or couch-sitting. Most likely, your energy has been consumed in a futile attempt to "herd the cats of daily eventualities." You have probably, with the best of intentions, been frenetically trying to singularly solve your every problem as well as be all things to all people. And yet, the fact remains, you refuse to surrender. Simultaneously, you perceive in the depths of your being, that there is far too much to be handled in solo fashion or by heuristic prejudices. *Just for today* may seem like an eternity!

The reader is respectfully asked to seriously permit yet another anecdotally stretched analogy which may be quite beneficial in exemplifying the above treatment. You are highly encouraged to keep an open mind while meticulously reflecting upon the following rather unusual illustration possibly representing your divorce experience.

Consider your "former life" to be a racked up set of tightly organized pool balls. This triangulated set was "broken" by your former spouse—the cue ball. Those pool balls will have scattered aimlessly in multiple directions. Obviously, they are no longer tightly organized as they randomly role over the entire pool table. Eventually, the pool balls do come to a halt in various locations on the table. However, once they have stopped rolling or bouncing off one another they are now in a state of inactive (inert) disorder or disarray. Those pool balls will never have the capacity to reorganize themselves into their exact original triangularly racked position. Unless, some external outside agent, has the energy, knowledge, time and desire to re-rack (re-triangulate/re-organize) those pool balls into their initial position prior to the original "break." However, even with the generous assistance of an outside agent, it is highly unlikely that each pool ball would be placed in the identical location that it was originally situated in prior to the "break." For example, the no. 2 ball may have had a front position but has now been relocated to the middle or the last row. However, the formerly disordered and disorganized chaos of the pool balls has been reorganized—only not in the unnecessary identical initial triangulated format. The original "pattern" is inconsequential to the re-racked pool balls since they are, in fact, re-organized for future activity.

If the patient and prudent reader will consider God as the external outside agent whose comprehensive ability profoundly desires to re-organize your life, this eccentric analogy becomes more intelligible. However, God certainly will not re-organize your life in its identical initial pattern, since this would both contradict history and impossibly regress into the former disorganization of your pre-divorced lifestyle. It also involves an infringement upon your inviolable free will. Rather, God as the omniscient, infinitely loving outside agent "steps into" your current new *just for today* life and intentionally refuses to replicate the former chaotic situation. God explicitly knows that you really do not wish to return to the identical disorganization of the past since now, your *just for today* life, even in its temporary exhaustion, is imminent. God implicitly knows that you genuinely desire and deserve a better, new and re-organized life. Therefore, just as those scattered pool balls most probably cannot reconfigure themselves of their own volition, God can and will. Your responsibility is to do those healthy, healing, self-motivating, *just for today* spiritual activities which will "get you off the couch." The gist of this tenth reflective analysis can be summarized thusly: you can manage any divorce healing concerns by utilizing a *just for today* attitude every day. God's enduring assistance longs for your petitioning to receive a directed and motivated guidance generated by the holistic spirituality (including human-divine interconnectivity) which you possess.

In the final overall analysis, you alone have the God-given freedom to either "lay on the couch" and await unanticipated divorce healing to discover and rejuvenate your entire being. Or you have the freedom to opt for a divinized strategic plan utilizing body, mind, and soul in nexus with the unconditionally omniscient God to energize and renew your life. The choice is ultimately yours, so also shall be the consequences.

CHAPTER FOUR

Really Loving Yourself

The reader who is absolutely determined to heal from the catastrophic effects of an unanticipated divorce is obligated to study this fourth chapter most conscientiously. Within its consecutive pages will be ascertained a profusion of advantageous considerations, penetrating reflections, and resolute *suggestions* each anticipating your aspiration to unpack and diligently apply their divorce healing relevance. Do not be aggrieved by the abruptly stringent and blatant delivery of this chapter's blunt resolve. Its direct approach intuits the reality that you literally waste your life as time to heal is diminished. Therefore, in a reasonable, responsible, and conscionable manner the fulfillment of the singular objective manifest in this volume for your divorce healing progress will be conclusively and rigorously submitted. The chapter's verbiage mandates an ardent, judicious and holistically spiritual approach as you advance cogently and determinedly toward divorce healing.

Now is the kairotic moment (the most opportune time) to earnestly move forward. It is the sacred opportune period for you to intensely realize that an appropriate self-love is an essential sine qua non in the efficacious divorce healing enterprise. Consequently, the entitlement of this chapter is neither facetious nor egomaniacal. It would be a flagrant violation of the principle of contradiction for you to regress and attempt an alteration of your pre-divorce historicity. Your life "progresses" forward in successive moments. Hence, whatever may have been your previous experience of "residuality," the intuition of chronology is flawless in beckoning the requisite fecundation to really love yourself.

You now possess a burgeoning new life. You, by the grace of God's gift of holistic spirituality, are the architect of this new life. You, with the triune God's guidance, design, fashion, and construct the new you. Recall, that you will no longer allow other human beings to define your being, essence, nature, or substance. While always in process of activating your potential to become more, you are never static even if metaphorically subsisting in some bizarre personality vacuum. Hence, a profoundly prudent yet unselfish love of yourself is absolutely indispensable for divorce healing development to transpire and endure. Engrained in our sociopolitico and religious culture the pervasive concept regarding the love-of-others has errantly over shadowed the very human (God-given) need for a healthy love-of-self. If one does not possess a humble, virtuous, reverential self-love (being made in God's image) a love of others is a feckless endeavor.

This chapter will offer multiple apropos divorce healing *suggestions* and observations for you to take responsibility in really loving yourself. In so doing, you further your divorce healing progress while simultaneously commencing the status of a new life. Therefore, the following material is mandated to consider your real self-love and its further development while articulating the divorce experience lovingly and professionally to any children, family, friends and the former spouse. However, as will continually be treated throughout this chapter, unselfish self-love is your imperative paramount priority. For if you are incapable of a healthy, healing, principled, God directed, love of yourself—how can you expect to give love to the other significant people (and the Deity) in your life?

Consider the reality that the term "love" in our culture has unfortunately become so banal that we use it for cars, clothing, homes, jobs, etc. This author, himself, must admit with substantial embarrassment that he has used the "I love you line" multiple times with the most remote sincerity. My deceit combined with an immature sense of "love" caused by foolishly succumbing to physical attraction resulted in a second unexpected and undeserved divorce and numerous decimated relationships.

The genuinely rational person while unable to define real love does possess an innate comprehension of the term. This is akin to the use of the term "time,"

Really Loving Yourself

of which we all *appear* to have a reasonably coherent understanding. However, we are hard pressed to define the concept. Nonetheless, it is intriguing that the grounded person has a multifaceted awareness of time and a penetrating desire to be loved.

Real love, from the perspective of this chapter is defined as an intensely deep-seated desire for the absolute good of another person. It is not merely a filial, family, or erotic love, it is the agape love of Christian self-giving encompassed by and within the Trinitarian Love. As this definition is applied to your ability to really love yourself, the interconnection should be obvious. You are categorically required, especially in the divorce healing process, to possess and demonstrate this intensely deep-seated unselfish desire for *your* personal absolute good. Without this understanding of real love, you debilitate the divorce healing enterprise.

Hence, as you meticulously study this chapter, recognize that your determined divorce healing objective is merely a pleasant wish unless it incorporates a strategic plan. Said plan is initiated in a twofold manner: first, through the adamant utilization of your holistic spirituality conjoined with the triune God. And second, by means of an honest unselfish appropriately Christian love of yourself by yourself and for yourself. This second element of the strategy not only supplements the above referenced holistic spiritual components (body, mind, and soul) but also affirms that you are indeed greater than the sum of your parts.

Really Loving Yourself

Since God is unconditional unrestricted Love and you are God's creation, made in God's image, no qualms should be attached to a healthy conditioned restricted love of yourself. You are naturally a finite being. Consequently, your self-love must have typical human conditions and restrictions. You and I do make "mistakes" in our loving endeavors. The effect of Original sin is one cause of our restrictions toward perfection in loving relationships. However, these factors present no rationale for you not to fully and virtuously allow yourself to really love yourself. Begin to love the person that you are today.

God would have never provided the impetus for your unselfish self-love if it were to be a cause of sin or patent narcissism. You were not created as a mistake but as an authentically magnificent human person. Simply examine your former pre-divorced life. A persistent lack of self-love may have errantly tried to consider giving all control of your very being to your former spouse, foolishly believing that this was true love. Doesn't this humiliation seem more "sinful," more a violation of God's omnibenevolent Will for you, than the real self-love that you are *now* striving to incorporate within your unanticipated divorce healing?

In order to properly and unselfishly love yourself, you must devote the necessary time and introspective energy to really know yourself. It is factually astonishing to realize how little one generally knows about one's self. How can you really love what you really don't know?

Do not skeptically ponder yourself into some circular logic—"I can't love myself because I don't really know myself." Or "I really can't love God since it is impossible to comprehend God." You and I love God because God loved us first. We have been freely graced with an holistic spirituality with which God permits us to penetrate, in an intelligible yet finite manner, sufficient knowledge of God's self-revelation through the Scriptures, Christian Tradition, and the Church's Magisterium. In a similar, yet not identical sense, this is also how we come to know and consequently love ourselves. It is God's grace that presupposes our human nature to appropriately, reverently and intellectually (utilize your mind, its self-knowledge, and its self-love) form a type of psychological human trinity. However, the implication is patently lucid as you examine yourself through quotidian experiences and focus on their import in both self-knowledge and self-love. In so doing you definitively progress in your divorce healing. As you introspect, you learn and love in healthy daily successive and progressive life experiences. Consequently, the physical exercises of your body, the intellectual exercises of your mind, and the candid prayerful communications of your soul, in focused interrelationship with the triune God expedite the procurement of unselfish self-love.

Holding an assiduous and coherent perception of the above will allow you to tease out both explicit and implicit notions regarding real self-loving demonstrable pursuits. This will become most revelatory as family and friends begin to express their observant recognitions of your development. When deeply personal serious introspection is conjoined with the God-given gift of holistic spirituality and finalized by the prudent comments of sagacious people your self-knowledge and self-love are enhanced. This tri-fold experience is further stimulated as you introspectively consider that the omnibenevolent and omniscient God creates only with, by, and through infinite Love. God desires for you to a have finite self-knowledge reflecting the infinite image of The Triune God who *is* perfect Knowledge (Christ) and Love (the Holy Spirit). Therefore, know and love yourself wisely and unselfishly, aware that God would have never created you without these gifts. Be assured that a tacit correlative integration must exist between your genuine self-knowledge and real self-love in order for comprehensive divorce healing to eventuate.

Simply stated, prayerfully ask for true self-knowledge and unselfish real self-love, and it will be given in due course as you faithfully follow your holistic spirituality. "Jesus, I trust in you, direct me toward an honest self-knowledge and a real self-love." The accessibility and potency of this brief prayer will augment your loving relationship with God and yourself.

Advancing this treatment, in the very practical and real world of an unanticipated divorce, the eager and sensitive victim, appears obligated to wonder "will I ever love again?" The answer is dependent upon whether or not *you* actually desire to intimately and unselfishly love again. Depending upon your personality and the Holy Spirit's direction, a devotion to the single life is an extraordinary gift unexpectedly proffered by your divorce. This enjoyable new life choice not only demonstrates self-love but allows for the freedom of self-giving to a multitude of others. Simply consider the life of a priest or a woman religious. However, the single secular vocation offers considerably more freedom and independence. It is not to be shunned and, in some cases, does ultimately lead to finding the perfect marital partner. However, a determination of this ilk requires profound prayer and an intensely acute self-examination, which by the direction of the Holy Spirit will evolve into a penetrating self-knowledge of your vocation.

The corollary consideration of the above question is absolutely contingent upon your priority to really and unselfishly love yourself. Far too often, we victims of an undeserved and unexpected divorce, errantly trying to fill the emptiness left within us, feel compelled to reassert our personal "attractions" by finding another marital partner far too quickly. This is a profound indication of an abuse in the rendering of a thoughtful self-knowledge and a sincere miscomprehension of an honest, unselfish self-love. These irresponsible and irrational self-aggrandizing propensities are the seminal reason for the currently huge percentage of secondary divorce situations.

Really Loving Yourself

Today, while this author is and will continue to be happily married (by God's grace and the assiduous use of my holistic spirituality), it is incumbent upon me to urge the reader not to confuse real self-love with both self-delusion and/or self-gratification. We can never find real love of self and its attributes in the frenetic haste to find it in another equally impetuous individual. This is specifically why really knowing who you are and really loving yourself carry such crucial implications. More unambiguously candid *suggestions* regarding these consequential issues will follow later in the healthy admonitions explicitly and implicitly provided further within this chapter.

Another stratum of really demonstrating direct yet unselfish self-love to enhance your personal divorce healing will now be considered. The reader certainly possesses a tacit awareness of, or has already been exposed too, the occasional inconvenient reality of interfacing with your former spouse. The objective of this critical segment of the chapter is to mitigate the "inconvenience" of this reality through stringent observance of the following proven seven *suggestions*. A conscientious study and application of these *suggestions* will elicit the maturation of your self-love to any observers. They will most probably astound your former spouse by demonstrating a formidable level of self-confidence, not previously apparent.

As always, begin any interaction, even an unexpected event, with a very brief yet sincerely potent prayer for infinitely guided Wisdom. A concise example, "Jesus, give me the right things to say with the right demeanor." Onto the following *suggestions*:

ONE

The less unnecessary contact with your former spouse, the quicker you will heal. Respectfully stated, ponder this rough analogy, if you wish to avoid the possibility of lung cancer, one method is to avoid smoking cigarettes. Unnecessary contact with your former spouse is often the genesis of resurging anger or a reawakening of suppressed romantic fantasies. Obviously, within some divorce victims, the possibility of recalled fond memories may emerge. This is not normative for all divorced victims. However, definitively emancipate yourself from any even remotely pleasant recollections. You are not eschewing your former spouse because of awkwardness, fear or intimidation. You are merely attempting to avoid the potential near occasions of bickering and further irrational disputes. Upon a first reading this may appear a cruel, non-Christian resolution. Recall, however, that even Jesus demonstrated a just anger and referred to the Pharisees as being hypocrites. Hence, at this incipient level of your determined divorce healing, focus only on the devastation and the ramifications of the ripple effect instigated by that former spouse. It is futile to dredge up past pleasantries or engaging repartee. *Your former spouse intentionally decided to obliterate the sacred, cherished, life-long commitment which seemed to give you meaning and purpose. Your former marriage has been desecrated by the former spouse and is now over!* This is the fact and do not allow yourself to rationalize its immensity. Recall, that you were the "residual," a leftover, selfishly and unexpectedly trashed for your former spouse's more provocative desires.

Hence, unless any contact with your former spouse is absolutely mandatory, appropriately avoid it. However, do not refrain from contact because of fear but through wisdom—the Wisdom of Christ, who tells us to "fear not." Interfacing with your former spouse in a context of fear rather than faith can only vitiate divorce healing progress. You have been working with incredible stamina to disengage and, with the triune God's guidance, establish a new life. Nonetheless, either in planned situations or by the laws of chance and probability, you will inevitably encounter your former spouse in "face to face" experiences or events. In these instances, your determined divorce healing attitude and strategic rehearsals, will demonstrate the new you. The Holy Spirit's guidance conjoined with your poise, self-confidence, and limited yet strategically focused rehearsed comments will astonish your former spouse and any observing "commentators."

Prepare for direct contact with your former spouse through brief yet potent prayer. You manifest control by setting your own time parameters, directing the agenda, the locale (if possible), and the guidelines e.g., no alcohol, no profanity, no provocative comments. Privately rehearse short polished confident statements making certain that you direct any conversation with succinct questions and assertions. Allocate the amount of time necessary to spend and then politely leave in a dignified manner. If this situation is not feasible, maintain your composure and deportment, by having well prepared yourself to endure. The above recommendations each require introspection and steadfast rehearsal. Quality musicians, actors, singers, etc., rehearse their performances daily. You must strategically prepare in like manner. Stand in front of a mirror and control your voice, facial and bodily gestures. Do not appear demure or uncomfortable but maintain an air of visible self-confidence. Challenge yourself through rehearsed self-speak, in the privacy of your home, to anticipate various contingencies and scenarios, based on your thorough knowledge of the former spouse's predilections. Adjust your strategic rehearsal to the event, the location, and the situation—e.g., she or he may bring the new paramour.

The reader, who keenly applies the above exhortations and guidelines in a mature, rational, responsible well understood and rehearsed manner will evidence authentic confidence and self-love. Indubitably both your former spouse and any attentively meddling gossips will be impressed by your extraordinary self-development. This will be the positive, healthy, and healing result of comprehending and exhibiting how to really love yourself. At the conclusion of these infrequent yet significant contacts, take pride in yourself and be thankful for God's direction.

TWO

Demonstrate real unselfish controlled self-love by never using either your children (if any) or family as pawns during this divorce healing schema. This *suggestion* may appear so inherently obvious that it is an exercise in futility to merely reference it. However, relatively probative evidence would seem to conjecture that violations of this mandatory rubric abound. As another effect of Original sin, divorced individuals possess an alluring inclination toward retaliation against their former spouse. Consequently, each party can become transfixed upon the most efficacious means or manners to anger and aggrieve one another. It is a pernicious game of foolhardy divorce brinksmanship which harbors a pervasive mental malaise while apparently providing some bizarre temporary satisfaction (which negatively impacts the children). It further develops into an onerous competition which maligns any healthy development and usurps healing time in an effort to construct the next devastating ploy.

While you have virtually no control over the machinations of your former spouse, you are responsible for yourself. Since you possess the God-given gifts of freedom of choice and holistic spirituality, the responsibility to react or not is absolutely yours. Even the omnipotent God cannot and will not take responsibility for your inappropriate and irrationally immature reactions. The reader should recognize that the act of taking complete responsibility for your actions is a demonstration of self-knowledge and real self-love. These assertions imply that as human persons demonstrate agape love by caring for another, one also expresses real self-love by holistically caring for one's self.

Hence, it is ingredient to both your real self-love and determined divorce healing, to transcend any temptation to misuse either the children or family as human leverage (carnage) against the former spouse. The deleterious effects caused by the separation of both spouses has already been sufficiently injurious to their psyches. The age or maturity of the children and the wisdom of any family members is inconsequential. The collateral toxicity is continually noxious. However, it can eventually be mitigated by your staunch effort to protect each of them in exhibiting, through appropriate actions, a genuine agape love for all concerned. *Despite all the accumulated anger, commit yourself at this moment, never to exploit your children or concerned family as pawns in a mendacious game of one-upmanship.*

When an effusion of strength is needed in this critical area, *you* must utilize your holistic spirituality and ask for guidance and patience from the omnipotent advocacy of the Holy Spirit. In issues of this nature, swimming in the water of the Holy Spirit is quite beneficial. Although actually drinking in the Holy Spirit's water is much more efficacious. Therefore, really loving yourself is often the result of an agape and a storge which is a God-given love combined with the love of family. This is engulfed by a love for "the potter" who molded, formed, and crafted you with, by, and through infinitely unconditional, unrestricted divine love.

THREE

Candidly taking total responsibility for all your behaviors toward the former spouse is an authentic demonstration of really loving yourself. This premise is a corollary drawn as an appendage to the previous *suggestion*. It is both an immediate consequent action and a logically drawn essential conclusion. It is considered as being authentic in the sense of its actual subsistence within the distinct human personage which you possess in a reasonable, responsible, and reliably rational self-understanding. Determinedly holding this "authenticity" of being, efficaciously illustrates your real self-love within the purview of the following three conjoined manners. First, you "define" yourself as a specific human person absolutely and uniquely created in God's image and likeness. Second, the existential fact is that you are a human person and, therefore, are innately capable and deserving of self-happiness, self-knowledge, and self-respect. Hence, self-love is inherently programmed within the very essence of your being. It is your personal birthright. Third, your holistic spirituality (body, mind, and soul completely interconnected with the triune God) imbues an originality of self that is immutable. You will always be you. Consequently, you possess a requisite congenital obligation which authorizes your uniqueness to really unselfishly love yourself.

Given the intricacies of the above, if your former spouse continually manifests an intractable attitude toward you, it can be assumed with reasonable certainty that her or his divorce healing efforts are most probably non-existent. Your self-loving responsibility is to consider her or him as a gadfly and hold steadfast onto the individual unselfish loving behaviors that you are currently adopting. Recognize, based on your previous experiences, that she or he may either be an envious provocateur or merely perpetuating an inherent selfish and ignorant predilection. Also, do not hesitate to consider that the former spouse may be bewildered and perplexed by your obvious self-development.

The scrutinizing reader, who is conscientious in the study of this chapter, should incipiently begin to deduce that one attains self-love by the elicitation of responsible behaviors. Taking full responsibility for all of your actions/decisions regarding the former spouse will educe self-respect and initiate an apropos and unselfishly necessary "falling in love with yourself." You become your own hero.

Rational human beings, especially the victims of an unanticipated divorce, wisely equate cognitively correct mental orientation with a healthy control of one's life. It is reasonable and responsible to envy a former divorce victim who leads a psychically composed and holistically spiritually controlled lifestyle. These determined albeit previous victims have arduously lumbered through excruciating tribulations with former spouses and in real self-love situations. They have discovered self-worth through taking full responsibility for their actions and decisions with a former spouse or any other self-love challenges. What they have done, you can also do. Consequently, strive to execute those tough decisions that will ultimately enhance your feeling of self-pride within the burgeoning *victor* that you are gradually becoming. The reader should introspectively recognize that you are graduating into an "achiever." You will no longer anxiously wait for "things" to happen. Now, you are going out and happening to things.

As you strive to really love yourself in the appropriate and unselfish manner that has been predicated above, the essential obligation to never prescind your holistic spirituality looms large. Recall, that Christ has said without Him you can do nothing! Hence, as in all divorce healing matters, the proper utilization of each component member of your God-given gift of holistic spirituality is mandatory. Offer your physical activity as a prayer, grant your intellectual stimulation as devotion, and donate your soulful actions as a benediction. A sublime prayer for abundant all-encompassing assistance to our omnipotent unconditionally loving triune God conjoined with your determined resolution in taking full responsibility for any involvement with that former spouse is an assured way to demonstrate real self-love. As we divorce victims, once residualized, attach our total fallen imperfect love to God's unconditional, unrestricted Love in petitionary prayer, you and I become absorbed within God's perfect love for all creation, including our very selves.

FOUR

As necessary, tactfully and transparently (through behaviors and very limited verbiage) disclose to your former spouse that her or his unanticipated divorce stratagem has opened a new life for you spiritually, mentally, and physically. Her or his selfishly evil ploy has, by God's providence, propelled you into a healthy, healing new relationship with yourself and the triune God. Reflect upon how the tragedy of your unexpected divorce is ironically beginning to reverse potency from its initiator to a newly stupefied victim. Formerly opposite roles are indeed being reconstituted and revamped. You now maintain control of yourself and this manifold effect is keenly apparent to any mesmerized onlookers. However, the marriage is over and you are not in a competition. The conscientious student can now readily observe that this transference is the direct result of the Holy Spirit's guidance in conjunction with your daily exercised holistic spirituality. The unique nature, peculiar evolution, and role reversal of this novel situation conspicuously signals self-assurance, real self-love and divine intervention. The fact is that in some mystically numinous manner God suffers with you while providing motivational inferences which draw your real self-love and divorce healing ever closer.

Given the significance of the above, recall that planned and well-rehearsed imaginative conversations must occur prior to any attempted explanation of this *new* you to the former spouse. Be conservative with your time and succinct in a sincere clarification, never permitting yourself to goad her or him as this may impugn their ego and consequently spur an unfortunate confrontation. Yet with sophisticatedly subtle actions and verbiage reference your genuine gratitude to the former spouse for this altered and pleasantly modified lifestyle through which God has used her or him as the conduit!

Per Sacred Scripture and the Magisterium of the church, you are a *new being in Christ* as a direct result of your baptism. Sharing this absolutely dogmatic assertion with your former spouse is essential as a declaration of your new lifestyle and as a "teaching moment" for her or his own comprehension and possible benefit. Demonstrate palpable pride in this gift, which is evidenced by your motivated and activated holistic spirituality. Celebrate in dignified, appropriate, and unselfish behaviors the reality that you are profoundly in process of transcending your old self. By your indefatigably determined divorce healing endeavors consonant with the triune God's grace you daily affirm this newness of being.

The reader, however, must be cognizant of and well prepared for, a highly probable denigration of your regenerated holistically spiritual personality evolution by the bewildered and perplexed former spouse. Her or his renderings may be multifaceted and present a plethora of criticism. The potency of envy will undoubtedly manifest its diabolic head as your independent holistic spiritual development moves toward a fait accompli. The overwhelming desire to incise both your maturation and patently obvious divorce healing progress will gnaw at the dejected spirit (often camouflaged) of that former spouse. The attempt to negate and trivialize your demonstrable new love of self may become a chronic theme in their discontent. You, however, must know them by the fruits of their actions and comments. In many cases, due to the cumulative effects of a self-centered lifestyle, perhaps, an innate narcissism, your former spouse has probably done virtually nothing in the genuine divorce healing venue. Therefore, she or he may be more confused and frustrated than you could have anticipated. Hence, their sole recourse is dependent upon a pervasively desperate and immature effort to purge their conscience by denouncing your success. You may be termed "a born-again Christian, a Jesus freak, or the crazy one who has now found God." The best response to this lunacy is the silence of considering the source and continuing to evidence your real self-love through the deeds of a tangible and daily exercised holistic spirituality.

FIVE

Focus solely on your new life in Christ and really loving yourself. Avoid the waste of precious healing time ruminating over the current life of your former spouse.

Really Loving Yourself

This concise yet practical segment unpacks into a series of rhetorical questions for your introspection. The reader is politely asked to conscientiously consider the above *suggestion* in reference toward your current status in both divorce healing and real self-love. Frequent candid reflections upon the following rather elementary yet profound concepts and questions will help maintain your determined focus when those occasional feeble times of fragility ensue. Extrapolate some vital conclusions from these following rhetorical queries:

Is the marriage and divorce over only on paper or in the very depths of your being? How is your self-speak really beneficial when you dwell upon the current lifestyle of the former spouse? Does it candidly make any real difference to you if your former spouse is or is not doing well? How does the success or failure of the former spouse have any genuine effect on your real unselfish self-love? How do you progressively heal without total focus on *your* daily life? Are you determinedly striving, on a moment by moment basis, to allow yourself healthy divorce healing progress? Do you fully realize and trust that immature curiosity is detrimental to your divorce healing pursuits? Why do you desire to increase the pressure which is currently present in your daily life? Are you authentically pursuing the Trinitarian God in all of your divorce healing and self-loving efforts? Finally, do you thoroughly comprehend that anger, hatred, and jealousy, are not as potent as being *indifferent* to the lifestyle of your former spouse as you pursue the unanticipated divorce healing process?

For the victim of an unanticipated divorce, the above questions, while rhetorical in nature, are very often at the core of a comprehensive healing. The reader is highly encouraged to deeply ponder their individual significance. They are not designed to be trivialized. Each can be quite purging of irrationally imaginative concerns while rejuvenating your focus and rationale to further pursue the divorce healing *suggestions* proffered throughout this book.

SIX

Prudent indifference to your former spouse fosters real self-love and furthers divorce healing progress. Correlative to the above *suggestion* is the final rhetorical question in that series presented for your most serious consideration. By way of reintroduction and concise explanation the thought shall be rephrased: *the opposite of love is not hate but rather indifference.* The caveat for this current *suggestion* is simply that this indifference must be prudent in nature.

For the victim progressively manifesting the ethos of "victor," while healing from the tragedy of an unanticipated divorce, "prudent indifference" may be considered an unselfish self-love sans concern for the lifestyle of the former spouse. One is prudent in the sense of a divinized wisdom which is vigilantly concerned about the safety, love, quality involvement and financial future provided by that former spouse to oneself, one's children and, perhaps, the family.

Despite the immensity of anger, frustration and hated which you may currently possess each of these negative reactions will eventually dissipate as your holistic spirituality is enhanced. Therefore, it must undergo an undeviating daily routine of exercise. Any remnant of hatred is an errant and desecrated waste of the precious gift of time and psychic energy which has freely been bestowed upon you by your loving God. Hatred only debilitates the hater and gives your unaware former spouse continued control over those copious efforts of the incipiently evolving new you. Recall, the natural God-given quartet of contentment found within your body. These are the neurotransmitters of dopamine which motivates you toward the action to achieve your pleasurable objectives. Serotonin, which, when released, produces feelings of your significance and importance. Oxytocin, which will aid in the creation of self-intimacy, trust, and binds healthy relationships (human and divine). Endorphins are available as chemical response mechanisms to anxiety, hatred, pain, and stress. Each of these natural gifts can profoundly counteract, through holistic exercise, the vitiating effects of not properly loving yourself.

Recognize that "prudent indifference" is the attitude that whatever the former spouse does or does not do, as long as it is neither injurious nor threatening to you or your loved ones, is meaningless. Clearly, you are obligated to condition your mind to fully accept this healthy, divorce healing reality. Your former spouse is now merely a tangentially and infinitesimally miniscule part of your continuously improving new self. This was the selfish, egocentric choice made by her or him for their unrestrained pleasure. Control this demonic endeavor from presently having even the slightest bearing or effect upon your burgeoning new life. Consequently, you are required to insulate yourself from her or his egomaniacal world view. Move forward by currently eliminating all former love of your ex-spouse and unselfishly invert that love entirely to yourself and the triune God. Hence, educate yourself through profound introspection on the advantageous nature of prudent indifference. As you evolve in the venue of prudent indifference and reject useless hatred, real self-love will become perdurable and divorce healing progress is allowed to advance.

Early on in this *suggestion* reference was made to your progression from "victim" to "victor." A word of caution is necessitated at this juncture. Certainly, no determined member of the unanticipated divorce healing community wishes to be labeled as a victim. Yet as the historical truth is candidly examined, you and I were both "victimized" by our former spouses' unexpected insistence on their urgent compulsion for a divorce. Hence, the use of the term *victim* is not meant as a derogatory definition of who you are as a person but rather as a term clarifying the result of another's psychically and selfishly abusive behavior.

This work never uses the term in a pejorative sense. It *was* your experience.

Technically, you and I are not really "victors" either. While you are progressing at your own pace in the divorce healing enterprise, there actually is no winner in this catastrophic machination devised by the former spouse. Consequently, continued healthy and positive development is most beneficial to your healing objective. You must persist in that productive direction. However, appropriate holistically spiritual divorce healing is not a competition. Again, there are no winners or losers, no victors and only one victim, you, in this realm of devastation. Resolve to expedite a real unselfish love of yourself through prudent indifference to the behaviors of your former spouse. Ultimately this focused thinking will mitigate and eventually transcend any divorce healing debilities.

SEVEN

In every association with your former spouse, remember where you came from, who you are currently, and the person that you are gradually becoming. This final introspective *suggestion* relative to both really loving yourself and strategic involvement with your former spouse deserves conscientious study. It is essentially a concise treatment of your personal evolution requiring a somewhat discomforting recollection of the past divorce situation. The next emphasis is immediately pursued by an adjacent contemporary view of your current life status. The balance of the discourse is finalized by a brief hopeful commentary on the graduated determination to actualize your comprehensive divorce healing.

Simply stated, the objective of this reflective *suggestion* is for you to realistically observe your incremental progress from "ground zero" to the present. Unmistakably, the above notions will compel the inclusion of some evocative yet illuminating rumination.

It is imperative that the meticulous reader return *her or his recollection to the type of person that you were* on the cataclysmic day that your former spouse insisted upon a totally unanticipated divorce. It was indubitably a surreal moment which immediately effectuated a total life alteration. The immensity of the disappointment and daunting shock cannot be verbalized nor imagined by one who has never experienced this deeply personal traumatizing event. There is no doubt that you were incapable of rendering any coherent rationale for your former spouse's aggressively assertive posture. Abruptly you were cast into the variant stages of grief. The denial, the anger, the bargaining both with God and your former spouse, the depressed attitude all eventually mutated into a despicable and loathsome acceptance of the tragic reality. Suddenly, absolutely unexpectedly, the world which you had become acclimated to had imploded. Now there existed only a very pale remnant of your life which had morphed into an ever deepening and complex enigma. You had become a mystery unto yourself. You were imbued with a suppressing reluctance toward engaging your world and yourself.

The haunting questions began to emerge and assault you like a legion of diabolic phantasms. "Who am I without my spouse? How can I continue to exist in this obfuscated condition? What will become of me, my children, my family, my friends? Does anything really matter any longer? When did my former spouse begin to plot this selfish machination? Why did I not observe its inception and attempt to squelch any metastatic proliferation? Where am I now going, as a real person, in my spouseless solitude? Since I am unable to focus on the necessities of life, am I losing my mind? How can I get revenge? I have dedicated my very self to loving my former spouse, is this the grand finale? Why did God do this to me?"

If these were reminiscent of the questions which perplexed you at the inception of the unexpected divorce declaration, there was minimal but significant solace to be drawn from the knowledge that you were not alone. You may have conceived of your divorce as the worst divorce in the entire history of divorce. Rest assured, we all initially have felt and thought in the same manner. However, no matter the circumstances or situations, your natural God-given proclivity to filtering out the negativities was, unbeknownst to you, embracing some level of healing. Recall that human time is non-regressive. Consequently, you have purged yourself of any falsity and ludicrous behavior, by ironically "embracing" the reality of an officially finalized marriage and divorce.

Really Loving Yourself

While it is a painful admission and a difficult proposition to reflect upon whom you once were, the application and detailed study of this book has proffered both subtle and distinctly obvious *suggestions* for your divorce healing. Hence, you are definitely in a much better position today by God's grace and your conjoined holistic spirituality. In fact, you actually are a different and a renewed person as of this very moment.

The *raison d'etre* of this chapter is to expedite an incrementally cogent analysis of your past, present, and future life styles. This approach will allow you to envision your personal development over time by replacing an ersatz love with a real candid and unselfish self-love. Only you can initiate the gradual mitigation of the effects of your past. This is accomplished by imbuing yourself with new, enjoyable, healthy and healing motivational activities. Understand that the efficacy and lucidity of this strategy is contingent upon the appropriate utilization of your holistic spirituality. Therefore, the proper use of your body as the temple of the Holy Spirit is required. The appropriate use of your mind in focusing upon those intellectual activities that stimulate interest is quite necessary. The candidly prayerful utilization of your soul as the venue that continually seeks God's healing directions is mandatory. This mitigation of past anguish will be highly productive and compulsory in your divorce healing enterprise. However, it is rarely an elementary endeavor and can occasionally be relatively consumptive of both time and psychic energy.

Yet akin to a vigorously disciplined work out at the gym, results (improvements) will definitively follow in time filled with a persistent strategy.

Reflect upon who you really are today. Are you really willing to love yourself enough that persistent effort in the radical change from your previous life is worthwhile? Knowing all that you have learned and experienced to date, would you, at this moment, be willing to marry your former spouse? Do you still truly believe today that the former marriage was your very life? Have you come to the realization, at this point in time, that you may have married your former spouse for a multitude of wrong reasons? Do you still conceive of marriage, today, as an institution of subservience, conditioned manipulation, and based on your views of idealized attractions? Do you view marriage, today, as a static condition involving very limited personal development? Do you comprehend, today, the absolute necessity for appropriate, unselfish self-love?

Your answers to each of the above introspective questions are invaluable. They are specifically oriented toward concretizing your actual self-evolution. You can readily observe the obvious development that has occurred within your mind-set and maturation of true marital understanding. Whatever may be your current circumstances or belief system, since human life is always in process, you cannot be the same person today. This brief but potent segment is illuminative. It allows you to self-analyze where you once were and who you really are currently. This comprehension should provide determined impetus in your desire toward continued progression both in self-love and divorce healing. Never disallow the reality of the triune God's direct involvement with your comprehensive growth experience. You will never be disappointed, negated, discarded, or divorced by your greatest and most ardent Lover.

Reflect upon who you are gradually becoming. Paradoxically, your unanticipated divorce, with all its anguished and hurtful complications has by the fire of God's unconditioned Love, begun to temper you like steel. Each day you are becoming a new and more fulfilled person. You are increasingly and moderately evolving into a holistically (body, mind, and soul) more accomplished, healthier and resolute individual. This is not locker room jargon or PMA hype. Consider and evaluate yourself in relation to the following developmental indices. "I am gradually becoming that person who:

1) Is much more independent and free to choose those things which are healthy and enjoyable to me.
2) No human person (in a relationship with me) will ever again be allowed to control my thoughts, words, or deeds.
3) I am becoming more aware of living through those necessities which will determine my divorce healing progress.
4) I am becoming incrementally aware of the Holy Spirit's involvement with my

interconnected holistic spirituality as the omnipotent aid in this divorce healing experience.
5) I can readily observe myself developing from a confused and frustrated "residual" into an authentic person who now desires existence in a state of unselfish appropriate self-love.
6) I see myself daily formulating and beginning to act on a specific direction in which to improve my entire life and that of my children (family).
7) Today, I am becoming ever more eager to live within my future and actively help its development."

If you can perceive a meager resonance with each of the above seven indicators, then you are gradually becoming a new and healthy person. In successive moments through the rigid temporality of your life the consistent forward progress can be observed and measured. The quotidian experiences of your life, independent of any need for your former spouse, will allow you by God's grace to strategically maneuver through the real world gradually becoming a new and healed person. Understand that the encountered life experiences actually have only a limited effect upon your "newness." However, *your reaction* to said experiences generates the additional and substantive majority of the holistic personality modification.

The following suggestive introspections are designed to encourage and reinforce your steadfast divorce healing development. As you candidly and conscientiously reflect upon each, remain adamantly focused on the essential necessity of both self-love and self-motivation in your incipient and continuous divorce healing. Further, profoundly analyze the prominence of your holistic spirituality (body, mind, and soul) interconnected with the divine auspices of God. These are the bona fide factors affecting who you are gradually and realistically becoming on a daily basis.

The ensuing remarks will each, in some obvious manner, require a mandatory praxis, which is a reflective action. They also insist upon a thorough self-examination of your authentic self-love and self-motivational activities followed by an actual demonstrative execution of these imperatives. Attentively ponder the following:

1) Your initial point of departure in this venue regards the concept of an appropriate and unselfish self-love. A generalized syllogism will be helpful in this cardinal matter. You are created in God's image and likeness. God is absolute goodness and Love itself. Therefore, you are created with, by, in and through absolute goodness and Love. Hence, real unselfish self-love is inate to your created being/nature. This is the very essence of that human person which is you.

Consequently, real love of The Creator God and yourself are a natural, normal and reasonable expectation.

2) As you gradually become the authentic person that you determinedly desire, learn from each post-divorce related experience. In eventualities with your former spouse, anchor yourself solely toward prudent endeavors, disregard the useless. You are an intelligent human being, fully capable of adducing and perceiving the demarcation between the sensible and replete nonsense. If this discernment should ever become complicated or tenuous, revert to the ever-present Wisdom of the Holy Spirit for impeccable direction by means of your candid directly communicative prayer.

3) Detail the categorically factual story of your unexpected divorce to concerned family and loving children (if any). Obviously, consider the emotional and comprehensive capabilities of their individual personalities. You will grow as you share the unadulterated truth, particularly without a denigration of your former spouse. Let each person draw their own conclusions and reactions toward this selfish catastrophe in their own manner and time. You, however, have freed yourself by candidly sharing your now cleaned slate. This will be a liberating and unblemished demonstration of your cour-

age to proper self-love by purgation without retaliation. Paradoxically, by genuinely releasing and sharing the old, you are deliberately becoming a new and vibrant version of yourself.

4) Present a positive expectation for a healthy, hopeful future for yourself and each of your loved ones. Demonstrate this by uplifting affirmations and constructive activities. Put some appropriate non-contrived fun back into all of your lives. By your actions you will heal and they will begin to realize and identify with this healthy new you. Clearly reference the multiple suggestions of this book and most importantly vigorously exercise daily your holistic spirituality (body, mind, and soul) to evidence an optimistic approach to life anew. "The Advocate of Hope" awaits your beckoning, therefore, act with hope to acquire hope.

5) During this developmentally incipient phase, avoid the temptation to acquire an "emotional" relationship with a member of the opposite sex who is, in some way, attractive to you. This is an extremely mercurial and precipitous area which despite its delicacy necessitates a compulsory examination. More will eventually follow on this critical decision and its aftermath upon your future and that of the children.

Whether you are a woman or man, every human person has the propensity and the occasions to be affected by the "broken heart syndrome." This, of course, for our purposes, is an extreme mental anguish which can demonstrate itself in curable physical symptoms—e.g., depression weight loss. It is relatively normal for members of the determined divorce healing community to suffer this syndrome temporarily and eventually, by means of a thorough utilization of their God-given holistic spirituality, to heal incrementally.

The elimination of the above "syndrome" can become obstructed or potentially negated when one who desires divorce healing relies upon her or his personal diagnosis and prognosis errantly attempting to design individualized coping mechanisms and strategies. This ill-conceived notion may include an obdurate resistance to one's holistic spirituality and prayerful interconnectivity with the triune God. It may also involve a blatant disregard for the many recommended and seasoned *suggestions* to be introspectively considered in this concise manual.

However, for those determinedly serious about dedication to a holistically spiritual (body, mind, and soul) divorce healing progression, do not attempt to find healthy healing in some immediate alacritous romance. Respectfully, yet frankly, you are not healthy or healed enough to pursue intriguing "affairs of the heart" at this particular developmental phase. Furthermore, since many readers have children, it is grossly unfair to them to bring another person into their lives until they too are comfortable, healthy, and really healing. This is determined by your honest communication with yourself and then by getting advice from your children (their age does not preclude wisdom). No medical doctor would allow you to rush your physical healing just because you are bored by the recuperative process. Even a nonchalant "date" may not be one healthy enough individual to engage in casual well-adjusted social consort. By continued prayer and deep belief in God's unconditional assistance for you, only then will an attitude of knowing not merely feeling healthy enough to *casually* date reveal itself.

If this is your current concern, impel yourself to cogently think without an obfuscated mind. Do not permit concupiscent desire, loneliness, or rationalization to become your Sherpa guides into a mountain of dangerously clouded or fogged territory. After careful study of this book, profound daily prayer for the Holy Spirit's direction, and the energized utilization of your holistic spirituality in quotidian events, you will become more cognizant of the true divorce healing process. At that juncture, evaluate yourself with absolute candor to determine if, in the most rudimentary way, you are ready for *a* casual date. Trust your gut instinct, it is often Spirit driven. Do not succumb to the temptation of envisioning self-love where only selfish love or concupiscence subsists.

Some of us in the divorce healing community (like this author) begin to panic wondering if our physical attraction and verbal repartee is in a state of decline or deterioration. Be assured, that this apprehension is ludicrous, you are in multiple ways becoming more attractive and conversationally more self-confident. When you are just "right," your human delineations and God's divine providence will conjoin to guide you to the "right," normal and healthy persons. Be respectfully advised, that you cannot sprint effectively on only one leg. The opportunity, as a free human person, does exist to convince yourself that harmless dating will advance the healing process more rapidly. This author's experience is painfully derived from the anguish of two unanticipated and undeserved divorces, followed by several failed relationships totally based on the allure of physical attraction. Today, by God's grace and the meticulous observance of my own individual and appropriated *suggestions*, in prayerful affiliation with an activated daily holistic spirituality, Trinitarian guidance has gifted me with the ideal marital companion for many blissful years. This came to pass when I knew that I knew that I knew that I was assuredly mentally healthy and thoroughly healed from the ravages of unanticipated divorce. In the same manner, all of the above assertions will be provided to you. Follow the Holy Spirit's directives in prayerful use of your intellect and will. Do not consume the potent cocktail of capricious desire as this will disorient your focus and detrimentally affect clear judgment.

If perchance the reader has already begun casual dating or is involved in a serious romantic relationship, the following respectful admonitions must be imparted especially if you have children (of any age).

ONE

Communicate candidly and thoroughly with your children (and reflect deeply within yourself) regarding their feelings toward this new situation. Allow them, if they are able to verbalize cogently, to emote and openly share their sincere apprehensions and queries. Converse with them (and yourself) through gentle, honest, non-threatening questions and give them your absolute permission to share any concerns or reactions as well as amusements or irritations. Aggressively listen for both disturbing idiosyncrasies and humorous observances. Seriously, take each of these under advisement, for from the minds and hearts of our children wisdom can be attained. Engage both yourself and your children in a spiritual manner, praying within the Spirit of Hope for a future of blessings and heartfelt peace. Hope is one of the theological virtues and is grounded upon Jesus Christ, the God-Man, who has endured all human suffering *and* did experience a happy family life. This is not pious jargon. Hope, so very necessary for both you and your family, is not merely a wish or a simplistic fancy. Nor is it a spiritual placebo. It is an ambitious craving for trust in Christ, your real Lover, who is gradually encouraging each of you toward a holistically healthy future in self-love and in "family love." As a reasonable and responsible loving parent allow for nothing precarious to transpire or permit no outside person to violate this precious gift.

TWO

Contemplate your precise intentionality within the purview of an apparently serious relationship. Do not become a casualty of self-delusion in a convoluted attempt to find love. Gingerly scrutinize your partner to locate any indication of disparate behaviors between her or his dispositions or proclivities and the divorce healing lifestyle that you are adopting. Do possible performance irritations appear to exist which you recognize in either her or his comments or mannerisms? Is it your hopeful intention to alter these behaviors? Do you visualize the complexities involved in even the most remote personality change? Is your libido orchestrating the clarity of responsible vision? Meticulously examine with forethought and hindsight the integrity of your partner. This need not be accomplished in a bellicose or churlish manner. Observation conjoined with "gut instinct" will provide a sufficient reminiscence of life experiences to distinguish the possibility of a healthy chemistry.

With keen attention focus on both verbal and non-verbal cues (e.g., inappropriate humor, overt interrogation, sarcasm, body language, boredom, impulsivity, and frequent phone checks) as these often intimate potential concerns. Recall that you are a work in progress, consequently the question turns on this indicator: where is she or he in their own divorce healing development? Do not become overly preoccupied with attractive physical or personality traits as this can obfuscate rational decisions and compromise your burgeoning value system. You are not being asked to live a cloistered, eremitic continuously celibate life, just candidly evaluate where you are currently and what is the intent of *this* relationship. Recall, *quo vadis*? Avoid creating unnecessary detours. Focus persistently on your single minded overall divorce healing objective. These choices are not for the meek and to abate them locates you in a defenseless position. The "Father of Lies" precisely comprehends vulnerability and targets an arrow of cupidity directly at your Achilles heel. "Evil personified" in cohort with his diabolic minions will use an ersatz materially sensual wisdom to confound you and your holistic spirituality. This is a devious attempt to counterpoise the Wisdom of the Truthful loving relationship which is only offered by Jesus Christ. The devil is evil incarnate and boldly tempted the God/Man. He will not be hesitant to repeatedly tempt you.

If the assiduous reader has not already done so, incorporate into the depths of your being the above recommendations. You have commenced a new life where the significant choices are made solely by your divorce healing determination in relationship with the triune God. No longer are your decisions coerced or tolerated merely to appease the whims of another. Consciously move forward with trepidation in the realm of a serious relationship as you are now the product of your own decisions. These thoughts are always truisms yet they become most applicable in the process of incipient divorce healing. Therefore, it should be patently obvious that a sexual relationship, whatever may be its allure and/or fantasy is *verboten*. However, despite this caveat many novices working through the divorce healing procedure succumb to temporal pleasure in an effort to momentarily assuage the pain of their divorce. Even more tragic are those members of the unanticipated divorce community who provide sexual pleasure to their current partner in an expectation that this distorted thinking will somehow maintain the relationship!

Notions of this nature reveal the reality that you can opt for healthy healing normal relationships or capitulate to carnality by either being used by or using another human being. Whichever may be the reader's current situation, you possess the God-given freedom and personal authenticity to adeptly rectify the predicament and progress *or* to errantly subsist in a convoluted state of illusion until the regression of your next "break up" comes to pass. Prudence dictates the initial option primarily because, in some sense, in choosing the later you are replicating the toxic and vitriolic embroilments of your former spouse. Your self-chosen virulence will quickly become lethal to an enormous amount in the unanticipated divorce healing effort.

THREE

The bottom lined concern for every reader involved in a serious relationship is: am I really thoroughly healed from the aftermath and ramifications of my previous marriage(s) and divorce(s)? "Ready, fire, aim" is frequently the illogical obfuscated approach that those dating too quickly within the unanticipated divorce healing community errantly entangle themselves. If this is representative of your current status, locate a place of quietude. Then, acutely analyze in a forthright manner whether or not this relationship is moving you toward or away from the real divorce healing that you have been studying. If you are uncertain, then you are not healed!

Whatever your gender, do not allow yourself to use or be used by another human being for purposes of ego or self-gratification. The person that you are dating may be marvelous in every respect. However, she or he is not the surgeon or therapist to heal your "broken heart" (which is actually an ill consoled mind). Only you with "the Divine Physician's" perfectly loving assistance conjoined with the Holy Spirit, "the Divine Counselor," will transform your divorce healing gradually and healthfully. Recall, that you will never again assume your holistic personality from another human being. You will love and be loved once again. However, this does not imply the resignation of your being to anyone except a *divine* person. God's miraculous power and unconditional love for you will make the "right person" crystal clear when you are healthy and amenable to make the appropriate physical and spiritual choice.

FOUR

In the privacy of a futuristic projected introspection, conceptualize the potential ramifications which may result when your current relationship has ended. Maturely consider your reputation and what has been undermined in the divorce healing process. Will you be stuck in the same mud once again? Do you fully realize that sexual activity, outside of a sacramental marriage, only creates more complications and confusion both during and after the relationship? Did you forego sacred intimacy for the "occasional" pleasured expectation at the conclusion of a typical date night? Can you really lay in bed with both your partner and the omnipresent Christ, Jesus?

    It is imperative for the reader to seriously reflect upon each of the above concerns, for it is a reality which most members of the unanticipated divorce healing community will be forced to explain both to themselves and their family. Think carefully about these issues today for they may be approaching more rapidly than you may anticipate. However, since you do possess a God-given free choice of the will, an acceptance or rejection of the above assertions lies within your purview. The pain of actualizing a commitment to your divorce healing, akin to many life-altering endeavors, is rarely comfortable. It takes considerable energy to move from the languid state to a condition of vigor. Yet for the determined member of the unanticipated divorce community who is engaged in an overtly serious or sexual relationship, ever more psychic energy must be usurped. Consequently, this belabored individual frequently chooses to do nothing, merely vegetating through a subpar, unfulfilling, debilitating, so-called, "relationship." Again, if this is your current situation, you have the authentic authority and divine support to professionally and tenderly draw it to a permanent close. As with so many proffered *suggestions* cautiously provided from divorce healing veterans, the final choice is always yours. Either you believe and can foresee these truths as progressing toward divorce healing. *Otherwise* your personal strategy must be acquiring clear and obvious divorce healing success. Think about your future, you can make it hope-filled or hopeless. Are you overextending yourself within an abyss of fallacious logic, impulsively and errantly attributing God's healing potency to your "current" paramour?

FIVE

If you are a Roman Catholic, have you contacted a respected priest to begin the annulment conversation? Christ, the greatest Lover you will ever have awaits you in both the sacraments of Reconciliation and the gift of Eucharist. Pursue a sincere dialogue communicating with a priest any concerns and desires regarding the reception of these God-given "signs of new life." Based on this serious discussion with an insightful priest, who may be found either at your local parish or through the diocesan offices, do not be hesitant to include your children and yourself in a weekly reception of the Eucharist, if canonically possible at this time. An eventual annulment will bring documented substantiated closure to your former marriage. It will nullify the former marriage

Really Loving Yourself

by delineating some unnoticed or unrealized impediment. It does not nullify your children's surname or the actuality of the physical event which occurred at the church. It annuls the sacred efficacy of the original union, which may have never actually existed. It is an act of freedom, self-love, and respect for God's intimate sacrament. It is never a matter of revenge. It is the revelation of some unforeseen or unexpected impediment, which usually preexisted the marital experience. An annulment is never a matter of shame. It is a self-loving act of wisdom. It is also a mandated canonical prerequisite necessary for the possibility of a future licit and valid Roman Catholic marriage.

If you are a member of a Christian denomination and not a Roman Catholic, consider the advice of a wise minister or pastor regarding your divorce, current lifestyle and the possibility of an eventual re-marriage. This communicative action is both emancipating and spiritually stimulating. A minister's or elder's sage advice is comforting and provocative as Christ's representative. A focused study of Holy Scripture's revelation is always mandatory.

Recall, without Christ, the God-Man deeply engrained within your daily life, you can do nothing to help yourself heal. The immense potency of this declaration cannot be underestimated! Always revert to your holistic spirituality, for sacred and infinite Prudence, to continually influence, yet never impinge upon your divorce healing freedom and progress. If and when you do stumble, rebound with more learned expertise and give your erroneous discretions to the Holy Spirit's pragmatic directions and guidance. Then through aggressively solemn listening begin anew to modify distorted behaviors and continually progress toward your divorce healing.

It is germane to the attentive reader's notions of the pertinent constituents presented in this relatively precarious segment that truly grounded self-love must proceed romantic love. Personal human self-love is our innate first love. All other human love is subsumed under our individual real love of self. For how can you really demonstrate love of another human person without an inchoate comprehension of self-love and an actualized unselfish first love of yourself? Recall, that real love is the consummate and preeminent activated desire for the absolutely pure good of another person. Without any sense of ego, self-centeredness or an obnoxious narcissism, you must love *yourself* in precisely this identical manner. Naturally, the above assumes a caveat of a non-extant propensity toward either cognitive or emotional impairments. Yet just as one cannot "see" material objects without the possession of eyesight, in an analogous manner, one cannot love without the facility to self-love. Whom does the newly conceived zygote love first: God, parents or self? Inherent within the original conception of this immediately developing embryonic fetus is the innately congenital conceptualization of self-protection resulting from self-love.

Ironically, as one truly loves another human person (e.g., parental love of one's child) this love is projected back to the original lover. In an authentically human dimension: I actually love myself as I simultaneously elicit true love for my child. Likewise, my child actually demonstrates self-love as she/he truly loves me. The healthy normal person loves to love and loves returned love because this action/reaction promotes self-love and is innately human. I love myself because I am capable of loving another. I love another because I am capable of really loving myself. Unselfish love is a reciprocity divinely incorporated into our human nature at the instant of conception. It is in some measure analogously akin to the relational love of The Immanent Trinity although on a most evidently finite human level. In this Trinitarian relational sense, the lover loves the beloved in the act of loving. The beloved returns love in a reciprocal act of loving the original source of love. In this dimension of reciprocity, the love freely given is so "loveable" that it initiates an overwhelming reaction which compels the beloved and the lover to love not only one another but also their very selves. It is the love of being loved. It is the love of loving. The love of the beloved is so loving that one is lovingly drawn into both a love of the other and the beloved. This action occurs in simultaneity and reciprocity between the lover and the beloved which consequently results in a mutual self-love and love proceeding from both lovers as the act of love. This is the innate self-love which is being referred to in this rather abstruse section.

If the above detailed explanation is correct, and if the reader is either involved with or seriously considering a romantic love, then two revelatory issues must be resolved. First, were both you and your former spouse really meeting the above criteria for a reciprocal and unselfish true love? Second, is your current relationship clearly demonstrating an appropriate total self-donation to one another while maintaining the requisite mutual self-love? Only you, the reader, have the emotional and reflective capacity to respond candidly in self-realization of the depth inherent within these core personal inquiries.

Hence, these two provocative questions provide a quality barometer to assess the nature of your former and current romantic inclinations. If applied with authentic veracity, each will be highly educative, teaching you much about your propensity to love and be loved. They will further demonstrate your need to really love yourself prior to broaching any romantic love interest. Incontestably, the above abrogates any sexual relationship. Since a genuine self-love must refuse premarital carnal knowledge in order to dignify its existence. Hence, reconciliation with unconditional Love Itself was earlier mandated.

Crafting out the quietude to examine the essence of love (which is the triune God), you will become more conscious (aware of your awareness) regarding the complexities and nuances, which this transcendent experience encompasses. In the transcendental nature of unconfined true love, you are accommodating the notion of what may be termed "numinousity." For the purposes of this chapter, love as a transcendent numinous episode is a type of relatively mystical humanly deified personal encounter.

It engages your unique propensity to disregard both space and time while incorporating you in a domain "outside and beyond yourself." Unadulterated love takes one beyond oneself because of its mystical nature. There is nothing preposterous concerning this explanation. It is especially obvious to those who have experienced an intensely true love yet have limited ability to explain the profundity of this potent emotion. Consider the reality that God is Love and that we in our finitude desire human love but are embargoed to eloquently postulate a colloquial and common definition. Frequently, the undetermined and skeptical member of the divorce healing community cannot abide a comprehension of love in this factual manner. It appears too abstruse and therefore desperately aberrant. For that unfortunate individual, love is merely inferred as an act of physical, material, tangible, somewhat sentient act of immature consciousness—an affectionate notion (e.g., "I love my car, my dog, my house, my shoes, and a good workout").

Your unexpected divorce has both consciously and unconsciously adduced as probative the grounded reality that love is, in fact, a numinous and transcendent experience. Your examined life encounters and the meticulous study of the recommendations and *suggestions* proffered in this book are ingredient to the incipient divorce healing progressing within you. The reader has most probably concluded that real love is vastly beyond any liminal mundane episode with a mere generic enchantment. An interesting and revelatory corroboration of this fact can occur with a simple yet profound self-assessment. Here is the proposal: the next time that you say, "I love you" to a relatively serious social escort, instantly and privately question your precise meaning behind this alluring declaration. Plumb the connotations, repercussions and tenor of your provocative articulation by immediate self-interrogation. Challenge yourself through the following queries: was this a statement directed toward a genuine agape self-sacrificing love? Was it a knee-jerk reaction? Was it a mere rapprochement of harmonious relations? Was it the conditioned response deemed as both polite and obligatory toward repartee initiated by your social companion? Or was it the trivialized pervasive exaggeration which comfortably misrepresents an ecstatic, responsible, sacred, unselfish locution of a perpetually maturating real love? Your answers will provide an invaluable self-teaching and self-learning moment.

The above questions do not intimate that you must never say, "I love you" to another person (human or divine) for the balance of your life. This would be preposterous! Yet it does force a specific posture relevant to the very title of this chapter. If you have assiduously inspected both the intrinsic and extrinsic significance of the "I love you" comment, then the astute reader is aware of the complementarity between self-love and love of God and family (children). Recall, the axiomatic assertions of this chapter. If you cannot unselfishly, appropriately, and in an agape (self-sacrificially giving) spirit love yourself first, then how can you give your authentic love to a potential future serious relationship with another?

In order to gently progress toward a corollary of those above introspective queries, probe yourself with the following revelatory analysis. Since my unanticipated divorce, have I actually tried to "fall in love with myself?" The reader may be somewhat astounded by this seemingly bizarre concern, yet, it is at the core of your divorce healing and its progress. It intimates nothing of an egotistical, self-aggrandized, inappropriate, sinful, or ersatz love. Rather this absolutely essential concern hinges upon the very first principle of human natural law for the determined member of the unexpected divorce healing community. This principle insists upon the activation of your innate God-given ability to first seek true goodness for yourself. True goodness is revealed in your desire to seek the healthy, healing, lovingly good, God directed inclinations for yourself and avoid the diabolic tendencies promoted by the evil of "the Father of lies." The very nature of the goodness implied herein is God. God is not merely good and loving. God *is* goodness and love itself. Whatever God has, God is. Hence, while you are unselfishly "falling in love with yourself"—simultaneously, your activated holistic spirituality assists your "falling in love with the triune God." Therefore, prior to sharing an "I love you" with another casual or serious dating partner always consider the following contingencies: 1) What is the authentic bona fide sincere meaning ensconced within this concise assertion?

Really Loving Yourself

2) Have you genuinely taken the time to first "fall in love with yourself?" If the answer to either of these self-reflective questions is flaccid, then you are not yet healed or healthy enough to pursue an outside relationship. Consequently, you are obligated to professionally, respectfully, and tastefully conclude this affiliation. Until you, a mature and rational woman or man, are absolutely able to truly "fall in love with yourself" despite any remnant of anger, guilt or frustration from your unexpected divorce, no serious healing progress will occur.

At this juncture, the reader may naturally ask both the why and how questions regarding this obscure concept of "falling in love with yourself." Substantive clarity of purpose and procedure is warranted to reiterate these consequential unanticipated divorce healing rubrics.

It is rational, reasonable, and responsible to "fall in love with yourself." Remarkably, it is a necessity in the divorce healing process for the reasons entertained below.

First, you have been created by Love, through Love, from an infinite number of potential possibilities. At the instant of your conception you were graced with a prodigious dignity of self-worth by being created in the image and likeness of God! This rationale alone should suffice. Hence, in appropriate, unselfish, agape, self-love you reflect God's love uniquely to the entire expanding universe. Second, since the God-Man, Jesus Christ, freely chose to suffer and die out of an absolutely pure love for you, your devout self-love is a modest yet appropriate response. God the Father, loved and treasured you unconditionally and desired your eternal reward by sending Jesus to die in loving obedience for the expiation of your (and all humanity's) sins. Third, recall the axiom, if you cannot love yourself how can you truly love another? This terse aphorism treats the reality that capability is contingent upon innate disposition rather than continuous effort. What is tacitly stated here is that without an initial cause there can be no consequent effect. You cannot give what you do not possess. Consequently, you must unselfishly "fall in love with yourself" before you are capable of giving true love to another human being. Fourth, a thorough sense of personal freedom is provoked when you forgive and love yourself by overcoming the lingering negative effects of any residual continuance to hold anger, guilt, or self-blame regarding your unanticipated divorce. Fifth, an unselfish, non-egotistical self-love frees you to be yourself authentically living in confidence and focusing on a healthy, healed, faith filled future. Sixth, no human person can activate an unconditional love—this can only emanate from God, who is Love. In self-love, you appropriately and naturally desire the very best for yourself. Yet the very best for yourself can only come by means of a self-transcendence and a fulfillment in love which is the deepest desire of all rational persons. This transcendent desire can only be found and fulfilled in God. Yet it is prompted by your love of self. You now deserve and desire the very best for yourself. Simply stated, this self-love generates your longing for the very best for yourself, which can only be discovered in God. You innately seek the ultimate highest good (God) for yourself, through your act of self-love. The above six reasons are sensible and probative in the "why" of "falling in love with yourself."

A treatment of the "*how* to fall in love with yourself" must now be specifically addressed. This vital area was considered in a fundamental manner earlier in the chapter. However, since repetition is the mother of learning, a specific and more coherent reiteration will be most advantageous. Adherence to this concept, particularly in light of the exigent nature of your unanticipated divorce healing is an adamant prerequisite. Focusing upon and stringently implementing the following practical recommendations in a qualitative format of committed praxis (reflective action) will be essential to your continued success regarding this critical issue. At this point of departure, the reader's centralized attention must be drawn to a candid self-examination. Now, this personal self-appraisal will be extrapolated by you in a non-intimidating and non-derogatory manner. It is designed for the typically average individual and is heavily based on the recurrent theme of your holistic spirituality. Recall, your holistic spirituality is that God-given gift of utilizing (exercising) the body, mind, and soul as components of the personality which you possess in an extensive interconnectivity with the triune God.

As previously detailed throughout this chapter, your self-love is innate. It is inherent to the very

Really Loving Yourself

nature of your being. Since, you are by your very existence a gift of God to the world, employ this "falling in love with yourself" concept immediately. How? *First*, by metaphorically standing naked before yourself profoundly consider each of your natural and positive attributes. This unprejudiced approach should be tantamount to a personal interrogation asking yourself what are the unique characteristics that I and others find within me? These should include all physical, mental, and spiritual gifts which you obviously possess. They should also involve those personal qualities, which only you are aware of, that are deep within the hidden treasure trove of your sacred inner sanctum. Candidly and conscientiously, accommodate even your most basic lovable character traits and achievements (e.g., raising your children or pushing yourself at the gym or your smile or your brief daily prayers or any characteristics that you admire in others that may be reflected in you). These and many more attributes can be discovered by not being either cavalier or reserved yet simply studying intensely your very self, from the inside and the outside, through the holistic lenses of body, mind, and soul. Put no embargo on this exercise—keep an open mind and see the fun involved within this healthy, healing pursuit.

Second, try to envision yourself as God envisions you. Absolute, unconditional, unrestricted Love itself has consummately "fallen in love with you." Therefore, nothing in this entire expanding universe should prevent you from unselfishly "falling in love with yourself." Again, this is done by the utilization of your holistic spirituality, offering its essence in physical, mental, and spiritual activities which demonstrate love of God and consequently, love of yourself. Enhance your relationship with yourself and the triune God by observing and *forgiving* in a non-egotistical manner the flaws of others. Ironically, respectfully observing and demonstrating indifference to the faux pas and wickedness of others toward you indisputably conveys the reality that you are truly blessed. To clarify the above statement from a most Christian perspective, you can honestly love yourself in a practical and sacred dimension by counterpoising your God-given gifts with the intentionally evil behaviors of certain others. "There but for the grace of God go I" is not a value judgment or a denigration of human beings who have freely chosen evil over good. Here, you are merely sharing with yourself in love the gratitude to God for the positive direction in which that triune God is encouraging your progress. All humanity is loved by God, yet some individuals unfortunately exercise their freedom by intentionally and knowingly choosing evil. "Fall in love with yourself" because you have prudently decided to please God rather than satisfy the cravings of a self-aggrandized ego. This condition of being blessed encourages and promotes, in non-judgmental discernment, your ability to fall in love with the goodness with which you are graced. There is no duplicity contained in this recommended exercise—more in this area will be shared prior to the volume's conclusion.

Really Loving Yourself

This relatively novel and somewhat opaque conception of "falling in love with yourself" is ideally becoming more transparent and less opaque to the studious reader. If this is not the case for you, do not hesitate to meticulously review and redline points of confusion. Then continue your reflections in the light of the unanticipated divorce healing progress which is a consequent result of this acute perception. Recall that with the non-interfering direction and Wisdom of the Holy Spirit you are never alone or stymied.

Moving forward, the *third* "why" in this compulsory trilogy will now be explicated. In unmitigated terms, the assiduous student of this chapter will intuit the blatant irrationality and untenable position of intimating a personal belief in the desire to be loved and to give love and yet not acquiescing to the logic of first "falling in love with yourself." The Promethean innovation expressed in this notion and verbalized in the phrase itself can be fleshed out into an even more palatable and simplistically delineated fashion. Hence, the reader is politely urged to give serious consideration in the deliberation of the following elucidations. Your point of departure will entertain a lucid and thoroughly encompassing definition of what has been meant by the repetitive dictum, "falling in love with yourself." Cogent comprehension of this precept is mandatory to further your determined progress in the unanticipated divorce healing enterprise.

The phrase "falling in love with yourself" may be specifically defined as the wholly appropriate, absolutely unselfish, Christ-modeled, self-sacrificing agape concerned, non-egotistical, non-ego-centered, rational and responsible, non-condescending, desire of the good for you as a human person. All of the above abounds in a finite yet definitive effort to unconditionally attempt a sincere self-love for whom you authentically are as that unique human being, a created masterpiece in the image and likeness of the one true God, who is unrestricted Love itself. For purposes of the fourth chapter, this precise all-encompassing definition is unequivocally, what has been the featured essence of an extensive treatment. It reflects the gravitas and magnitude of this absolutely necessary concept.

Diligently introspecting upon the above expanse of unambiguous and reasonable assertions, in this final analysis, the reader is respectfully admonished not to merely ponder the definition but to assertively embrace the oft *suggested* paradigm. Buoyed by the potency of the Holy Spirit in direct interconnection with your God-given holistic spirituality, *just take a leap of faith* and "fall in love with yourself all over again." Beyond question, you know the truth of yourself more profoundly than any other human being. You alone candidly know the real gifts that help make your personality unique and desirable. You alone fully comprehend what your heart has to offer. You alone know, with full conviction, from "Whom" everything that is so positive about your very being has been lovingly entrusted. Therefore, knowing all of these God-given treasures, do not be hesitant to rebuke and relinquish the plague of negativity which will diabolically try to infest your self-worth. You are categorically capable of publicly decrying and personally transcending any evil induced and demonically driven nonsensical persuasions. The "father of lies" would delight in titillating your inclinations to find flaws or inadequacies within yourself. This evil spirit is very real and is laser focused on pulling you into an abyss of believing in your unworthiness to love yourself or others unselfishly. This debilitating approach centers upon demeaning your physical attraction, mental acuity, and emotional/spiritual stability. However, recall that since your body, mind, and soul are grounded in God's Holy Spirit, you can only succumb to these inaccurate criticisms by an errant free choice of acceptance. Simply effectuate your repulsion of them in accord with a pronounced acknowledgment of who you really are and what is your ultimate goal. Then, progress in your divorce healing enterprise by immediately and continually conjoining the holistic spirituality that you possess with the triune God's unconditional Love.

The point of all the above is that each of us, made in God's image, love because God is Love and it is inherent within our lovingly created human nature. Consequently, when you and I really love ourselves, appropriately and unselfishly, we are both doing God's Will and finitely imitating God's nature. Herein we members of the unanticipated divorced community find the ideal point of departure for our divorce healing. Love of God implies love of God's creation which further implies *really loving yourself.*

EPILOGUE

The intent of this concise volume has been to passionately incite your determined desire to heal from the emotional, psychosomatic, or psychological abuse and anguish prompted by an unanticipated undeserved divorce. The methodology required arduous effort to follow pragmatically proven principles consummately designed to attain your challenging ambition. One procedure used was to imbue the earnest reader with a cascade of intimations, recommendations, and both subtle and obvious *suggestions* ingredient to her or his unforeseen divorce healing endeavor.

A correlative segued approach was presented through viewing the loving invitation of the triune God for you to make thorough recourse to the inherent holistic spirituality innately presupposed at your conception. Emphasis has been placed throughout the presented material on the incongruity and associated futility of your healthy unexpected divorce healing without the petitioned intervention of the Trinitarian God.

The concept of holistic spirituality, for purposes of this study, consists of your human body, mind, and soul as the tangible, perceptible and transcen-

Epilogue

dental components which are oriented in a type of theological anthropology interconnected with the tri-personal God. This relatively complex yet novel view of traditional spirituality subscribes to a view of the "wholeness" of human spirituality by emphasis on a less banal and flaccid comprehension. As has been explicated in previous chapters, it seeks to advance the divorce healing process more efficaciously by actively exercised and motivated utilization of the entire authentic human person. This tenable approach is further enhanced by an absolutely necessitated interconnectivity with the divine designer, creator, and sustainer of each unique individual as created in God's holy image.

The implications unpacked in your study tacitly imply that although anger, confusion, and frustration are existentially present as normative response to the gravitas of an unexpected divorce experience. You are impelled to pursue an incrementally progressive healthy healing experience. This palpable dedication when conjoined with the grace bestowed by the Trinitarian God provides a myriad of potent *suggestions* which will help mitigate your grief.

The intimated strategy has been to intentionally place the onus upon you to correlate your healing within the purview of divine omnipotence and omniscience. As previously clarified, this notion is not some cobbled together disingenuous pious platitude, designed to allure the needy or mercurial member of the unanticipated divorce healing community. Rather, it is the realistic counterpoising of a replete strategy to move the confounded novice (of any age) from a "residual" and "victim" to an authentically formidable untethered human person.

As a consequence of the above, and in fulfillment of the divorce healing process, a comprehensive utilization of your holistic spirituality must be a quotidian endeavor. This implies devoted application of your componential entities (body, mind, and soul) to the proposed unanticipated divorce healing schema. Since each human person is uniquely made in God's image and gifted in variant ways, the acuity which they possess regarding their holistic components will also naturally vary. Some people simply possess a greater propensity, skill level or ability than others to utilize their physicality as prayer to the Trinity. The same concept holds for those more intellectually or soulfully capable of using these components as perceptive and spiritual enhancements.

However, as has been *suggested*, minimal attention is given to your personal human talents. Every individual is required to merely engage her or his holistic spirituality according to their level of competence. This procedure will initiate reliance upon the very nature of the Holy Spirit as your personal omnipotent, omniscient, divine therapeutic Counselor.

Naturally, as this volume has also *suggested*, other members of the unanticipated divorced community have become suspended within an anemic and/or lethargic apoplexy. Their assiduous study of this concise book and genuine application of its principles and *suggestions* is mandatory in the attain-

Epilogue

ment of necessitated self-motivational techniques. Additionally, and in conjunction with the proponents of passivity, multiple others have resorted to the denial of God's existence in order to mitigate, through errant rationalization, the anguish they continually endure. These improprieties while deleterious are real and relatively commonplace. They require a more thorough grounding in the reality and unconditional love of the triune God as postulated throughout the treatment of each chapter. Therefore, more prayer, study, and application are obligatory for the skeptic to procure healthy divorce healing results.

Whichever of the above categories may be your current status you have been graced with the freedom to choose atrophy or dynamism in confronting an unanticipated divorce healing. As previously stated, you may freely choose to deny the exercise of your holistic spirituality, and cede to chance, fate, luck, serendipity, perchance the vague issue of time for divorce healing. Or as encouraged throughout each chapter, you may freely elect to capitalize on *suggestions* from this book in conjunction with your holistic spirituality interconnected with the omnipotent, omniscient God. With either choice, your holistic spirituality continues to exist either as actualized or in dormancy. You must ultimately choose to adopt the God-given strategies available for healing or merely vegetate on the uncomfortable couch of illusion. In the realm of your inherent desire for unforeseen divorce healing no other choice exists. Follow the successful pursuits of many formerly angry, con-

Epilogue

fused, and frustrated veterans who have, even in the throes of heinous desperation and exhaustion, persisted until they fully realized that their unanticipated divorce healing goal was achieved.

For those dubious about the material shared within this book, remember, that the reality of an inverse proportionality is always in effect. The more that you rely only on yourself for genuine unexpected divorce healing the less healing will be experienced. Conversely, the less that you expect from your own concocted schemes and the more dependence fixated upon God's collaboration, through your holistic spirituality, the greater will be the healing progress. Rendered in another fashion, the more God is involved in your unanticipated divorce healing, the less likely you are to vitiate that healing process.

Given the above axiomatic assertion, whatever may be your current disposition, an assiduous study of this book (not merely a perfunctory reading) conjoined with daily praxis (reflective action) and application of your holistic spirituality is ingredient to healthy unanticipated divorce healing progress.

The "laws" of probability, or the occasions of happenstance, the inclinations of serendipity and the aggregation of time while existent realities are feckless in the spiritual matters affecting a demoralized heart and an obfuscated mind. The informed and determined reader must exhaust no more of her/his life pondering the past or an illusory future. Waste not another moment of your existence on contemplating the current activities of the former spouse. If

Epilogue

you do so, then "chasing the wind" has become your delusive endeavor.

Focus with laser precision, using the God-given holistic spirituality which you possess, on applying the principles and *suggestions* found throughout this treatise. Conscientiously review each chapter under the umbrella of God's unconditional, unrestricted Love and determinedly desire to affect your positive divorce healing progress. Recognize that all healing from grave injury is alleviated through the stamina of the injured and the skill of the physician.

A conclusion crafted as useful for the reader must follow a procedural schema, which compels an inner dialogue to emerge based on reflective questions evolving from each preceding chapter. The intent, then, of the following salient *considerations and questions* is to induce an ever-deepening insight and understanding of the unanticipated divorce healing process as promoted in this book.

1.) Notwithstanding the probability that you are emotionally drained and overwhelmed by the ramifications of your unanticipated divorce, the architectonic structure of this book while adding incremental stress is essential to a healthy holistic healing enterprise. The old saw, "no pain, no gain" is highly applicable in an endeavor of this magnitude. Ironically, one of the initial indicators of your divorce healing is the desire to adamantly pursue the intended

Epilogue

objective when you are most weary. "Flagrant fortitude" is a gift of the Holy Spirit and your newest mantra. In the culture of death which seems so pervasive, we applaud the success which seems to appear only nanoseconds prior to one's complete loss of patience and persistence.

2.) Given the above assertion, are you absolutely determined to *accomplish all* that is required to heal in a healthy holistic manner from the detrimental effects of your unanticipated divorce? Your candid response to this direct question locates or removes the sole responsibility for an initiating of divorce healing upon you! This is the "quo vadis" question in a hauntingly diverse format.

3.) The following factors comprise *your strategic plan* for a dynamic healing from the catastrophic impact of an unanticipated and undeserved divorce. The implementation of this strategic plan holds you accountable to yourself in the resolution of your healthy divorce healing enterprise. Therefore, execute the subsequent propositions with a lucid understanding and a determined response.

A) It is mandatory to comprehend the fact that neither you nor God is responsible for the occurrence of your unanticipated and

Epilogue

undeserved divorce. This egregious decision was the freely willed heinously despicable choice insisted upon by the selfish narcissistic inclinations and impulses of your former spouse.

B) Only you can ascertain the positive new direction in which your life must now flow. If your preference is an obdurate avoidance of this healthy endeavor it will be tantamount to eking out an aimless existence engulfed by futile effort. Although this notion (of a positive new direction) will necessitate weighty reflective contemplation in order to grasp the remarkably ironic fact that good is being drawn from evil. You have been proffered the opportunity to live an independent, new, rich, and uncompromised life resulting from your unanticipated, undeserved divorce! Undoubtedly, some readers will view this insight as opaque and a preposterous stretching of reality. However, the astute reader, receptive to an invaluable premise, will ascertain this novel paradigm as a potent truth advancing unanticipated divorce healing progression.

C) Without exception, you are compelled to "exercise" your holistic spirituality on a *daily* basis. This imperative means what it states and states what it means since it is the crux of your *strategic plan*. You must physi-

Epilogue

cally activate your body each day. You must mentatively stimulate your mind daily. You must prayerfully entreat the triune God by means of your soul's communicative invocations every day.

Recall that these components are your holistic spirituality and when exercised become a prayer which requires a daily interconnection, a palpable interrelationship with the unconditional and unrestricted Loving God. Consequently, not only will these componential exercises vitiate the doldrums of your divorce, but also they will increase physical, psychic, and spiritual energy. They allow you to use your entire being as candidly exerted prayer. This prayer, which is communication with God, can be angered, seeking guidance, thankful, or petitioning resolve during periods of difficulty. As previously mentioned, aggressive listening for God's response through other people, situations, or daily experiences is of paramount significance in this *strategy* which will promote healthy divorce healing progress. Reliance upon the Holy Spirit, coequal and consubstantial with the Father and the Son, and therefore omnibenevolent, omnipotent, omnipresent, omniscient, is absolutely warranted for the prudently determined member of the unanticipated divorce healing community. God, the Holy Spirit, "the divine therapist" awaits and responds to your daily communiqués through the efficacious "exercises" of your holistic spirituality. You will be trapped within a vortex of

Epilogue

obfuscation without this daily direction and guidance of the Holy Spirit.

D) A constituent element of your strategic plan is the daily committed effort to implore God for the execution of a divorce healing miracle. It is categorically beyond contention that God can, has, and does perform miracles. The circumspect reader will recognize that life, and the most intricate universal particles, as well as this entire expanding cosmos with all its constituents are an observational miracle. We are ensconced in quotidian miracles. Yet the fact is that the omnipotent God will not miraculously alter the historical event of your unanticipated divorce. God does not regress time nor infringe upon the free will provided to your former spouse in her/his initiation of divorce proceedings. God will not apply miracles through contradictory states. Explicitly asserted, for the reader's strategic planning while simultaneously encompassing the unanticipated and undeserved divorce healing enterprise, is the fact that God cannot alter the historic reality of your unanticipated and undeserved divorce. However, by the prudent daily exercises of your holistic spirituality as interconnected prayer to the triune God the implored miracle will come into existence as a positive, healthy, healing *change within you*! The significance of this miracle can never be underestimated because it will gradually mitigate and ultimately eliminate your current anger, anguish, confusion, and frustration. This is the miracle that is really to be sought by your directed holistic supplication for a comprehensively omniscient response through God's foresight knowing what is best for you. Herein lays the real miracle.

A metanoia, a complete and thorough change of your heart and mind, moving you closer to an extensive divorce healing. Therefore, do not restrict God by an obstinate utilization of your free will. Do not abrogate the real miracle by denial or exclusion of this strategic proposition. Through a faithful dedication to the explicit and implicit *suggestions* shared throughout this book, and the potent supplementation of your daily exercised holistic spirituality interconnected with the triune God, the appropriate miracle will materialize. You alone must "allow God into the real situation." The profundity and duration of the miracle's manifestation is entirely within your possession. Hence, if you are unambiguously devoted to faithfully observing this strategic plan in coordination with the daily exercises of your holistic spirituality God-given miraculous changes will become apparent. You are able to determine the success of these factors upon the tragic unanticipated and undeserved divorce healing by monitoring the mitigation of the pent up negativity which formerly possessed your being. However, the tendencies of carnality, despondency, and lethargy contain diabolic potency. Consequently, *when* you err, learn from these experiences do not subvert the miracle. Next, immediately refocus your thinking and actions toward the application of the healing behaviors which you have been assiduously studying.

E) Succinctly stated, this strategic plan is correlative with the overarching success of your unanticipated and undeserved divorce healing. Therefore, impel yourself to acknowledge the following proposition. From this point forward, maintain a substantially prudent and respectful *indifference* toward any unnecessary concerns regarding your former spouse. The success or failure rate of your former spouse should be of no consequence to you. Recall, that when you consider the life events of your former spouse an unknown "control" is being surrendered to her or him. You debilitate the determined attitude never to cede your new life and personal authenticity to another human person. Oddly, that other human person is most probably totally unaware of her or his dominance over your thoughts and feelings. Demand control of your errant curiosity by continually committing to a healthy, healing, holistic strategy of respectfully prudent indifference. This type of indifference is virtuous. It does not imply a "Spock-like" (stoic) absence of emotional neutrality. It does not desire either good or evil upon the eventualities of your former spouse. Consequently, it allows you to adamantly focus on your aspirations, self-development, and divorce healing progress. Do not relinquish your incipient self-control in envy or jealousy to some real or imaginary erratic notions attributed to the former spouse. In actuality, how does the failure or success of your former spouse affect you? Obviously, if alimony or child support or visitations are obligated by the court then become meticulously diligent and proactive in your concerned awareness. Further, if serious illness or death were to befall your former spouse you must maintain a respectful and prudent indifference holding to your Christian values while not succumbing to either vengeful thoughts or romantic illusions. In sum, a resolute yet respectfully prudent indifference toward the circumstances of your former spouse is critical to this strategic plan and consequently to your healthy holistic divorce healing progress.

F) It would be incongruous to implement a strategic plan without including the real-

Epilogue

istic possibility of *hope* for your successful future. Since the future is dependent upon the present, you are obligated to incorporate a genuine sense of hope into your divorce healing agenda. Hope is not a wish, a daydream or a capricious fancy. Hope, for all members of the unanticipated and undeserved divorce community who are determined to heal, is a living entity. It osmotically develops as your healthy holistic healing interacts with that God-given holistic spirituality and a devout interrelationship with the Trinity. Hope, like faith and charity (love), is a theological virtue. Consequently, it is also an anthropological tendency to live a life oriented toward happiness. Humanity's ultimate happiness is only found in a fulfilling eternal relationship with the triune God. However, even the atheist, the moral relativist, and the secular humanist, desire happiness and this corresponds to a hope-filled present and future. The primary method for incorporating hope into your burgeoning new lifestyle is to palpably internalize your personal self-progression. Observation of your current incremental successes in the divorce healing process, while clearly focusing on a hope-filled future and *sharing* that hope with loved ones exponentially increases this theological virtue within all concerned individuals. Hope can be perceived as the prime "attitude adjuster" of both heart and mind when the doldrums negatively impact your determination to heal. Consequently, the pursuit of hope, especially in times of tribulation is a formational requisite activity of your strategic plan and, therefore, interconnected to the healthy holistic divorce healing process. Finally, one of the additional benefits of hope is the joy (fun) that you manifest throughout the course of the day. There is no hope based edict or formula which insists upon maintaining a glum disposition in the presence of colleagues or loved ones. Hope is naturally contagious and attracts others to you as its initiator. People enjoy being in the presence of truly hopeful persons. As you gradually observe this inspiration in your daily life, it will radically enhance the qualities of self-love and self-motivation which foster a continued unanticipated and undeserved divorce healing momentum.

G) The culminating and most radical constituent of your strategic plan, indeed, the apex in the determinedly efficacious divorce healing enterprise, may expose itself as both incoherent and preposterous. It resides within your proficiency to *forgive that which appears unforgiveable*. The reader is obliged to distinguish between the acts of forgetting and forgiving. It may be a physiological impossibility to forget the trauma of your unanticipated and undeserved divorce. However, while forgiveness may be immensely difficult to envision and assimilate during the "developmental moments" of your holistic divorce healing, it is the only method to unequivocally release control by your former spouse. Consequently, allowing yourself to enjoy the unencumbered freedom of life anew.

The complexities of forgetting tacitly proffer a repressive behavior which is indicative of a stringent resistance in permitting one's self to avoid entertaining the traumatizing feeling provoked by a devastating event. To date, this author has not encountered a single member of the unanticipated divorce community who evidences this capacity.

However, if one perceives forgiveness as the action (s) which assuredly will not tolerate any further harboring of anger. This thought content may illuminate a necessity which is both rational and possible.

Initially, the above concept of forgiveness, while not readily palatable, instigates the notion that one's forgiveness of an apparently unforgiveable person or experience culminates in a healthy healing objective. Recall, endeavoring to "hold a grudge" only vitiates you (and your loved ones) while simultaneously ceding the acquiescence of control to your former

Epilogue

spouse. Prolonged acrimonious inclinations exacerbate diabolic tendencies and exigently constrain healthy divorce healing advancements.

If forgetting is impossible, forgiving is a necessity in providing the absolute closure toward all the divorce related anguish previously endured. Through the God-given grace of your holistic spirituality, aspire to absorb and emulate the crucified Christ, who forgives the ignorant for their despicable machinations and cruel behaviors toward Him.

The act of forgiveness, a divinized consideration, may currently continue to appear ludicrous. However, forgiveness toward your former spouse, will manifestly release any residual anger, permit prudently respectable indifference, and promote the freedom obligatory in a newly energized life. If you permeate your time with profoundly reflective prayer and a focused sense of logic then forgiveness will become the only reasonably Christian conclusion.

In a requisitely abrupt interrogative analysis, as this book prepares to conclude, assuredly every normal person who has experienced an unanticipated and undeserved divorce desires to be healed. Assuming that this is the intent of the reader, the following questions necessitate examination and resolution.

Are you thoroughly willing to exert the compulsory effort expected by the successful attainment of a healthy divorce healing challenge?

Despite your current level of psychic exhaustion, are you capable of a profoundly candid self-transpar-

Epilogue

ency and a rationally attitudinal approach toward conclusively asserting an unwavering determination to abide by the recommendations, strategies, and *suggestions* proffered in this concise manual?

Do you faithfully concur with the mandate to exercise your holistic spirituality (body, mind, and soul) and its trusting communicative interconnectivity with the Trinitarian God on a quotidian basis as a genuine necessity in the divorce healing process?

Can you categorically affirm a stalwart belief in the unconditionally, unrestricted God's creative agency, infinite Wisdom, and omniscient inspirational direction as the only reliable and absolutely Truthful source of your unanticipated, undeserved divorce healing?

An unyielding acceptance of these four questions demands that you no longer endure another nanosecond of your former lifestyle. Trust in God and yourself, then, immediately begin to achieve your unanticipated, undeserved divorce healing objective.

ABOUT THE AUTHOR

Dr. Milton Michael Kobus was born and raised in Chicago. He attended seminary and there earned a BA in philosophy. His education was furthered by graduate degrees in both education and theology. Dr. Kobus then attained a doctorate in theological studies. He has taught and administered at elementary, high school, and university levels. Dr. Kobus has lectured and written extensively on the holistic divorce healing process. He is very happily married and boasts two sons and two young grandsons. Dr. Kobus has a profound desire in assisting women and men who have been devastated by an unforeseen and undeserved divorce. His proven methodology for unanticipated divorce healing involves the appropriate usage of the victim's body, mind, and soul. While he works at his own spirituality, his writing involves no pious platitudes. Rather he tends to proffer practical, real-world strategies and suggestions which insist upon the interrelationship of the components of the whole person utilizing divine assistance.

Dr. Kobus is available upon request to facilitate discussion groups or seminars regarding the Unanticipated Divorce healing process. He may be contacted through his email, drmkobus@gmail.com